# I was born "pretty"

## PLEASE BE PATIENT. PLEASE BE KIND.

Jimmy Belasco

ISBN (e-book): 979-8-9940027-0-4
ISBN (paperback): 979-8-9940027-1-1
ISBN (hardcover): 979-8-9940027-2-8

Library of Congress Control Number: 2025926018

Published by theJiMMYtalks in Dallas, TX, USA
Printed in the United States of America
Second Edition, 2026

Cover concept & art direction: Jimmy Belasco
Design & layout: M. Mahbub Alam
Cover photograph: Belasco Family Archive, c. 1966
Photographs: © James Belasco and the Belasco Family Archive, except where noted.

*For my dear, dead Mom—*
*You showed me love without limits...*
*and that the best laughs live just beyond the edge of good taste.*

*I may have been born "pretty"—but I know what love is.*

—Jimmy Belasco

# Introduction

I was losing my mind—not in a fun, Boys-Gone-Wild-and-barely-legal kind of way, but in a two-years-of-caregiving-during-a-pandemic-while-Mom-was-dying-left-me-Coo-Coo-for-Cocoa-Puffs kind of way. After she passed, I had precisely one marble left. And it was cracked—along with the rest of me.

I needed to get out of that house, or we'd need a bucket of holy water to reverse the damage.
So, I did what any emotionally stable person would do: I got in my car and drove—and then kept driving.
For six months.

What started as a short escape became something much bigger—a *Forrest Gump*-style accidental tour of the country, coast to coast, top to bottom. Instead of strapping on some Nikes, I strapped myself into my car. No real plan—just a quiet hunch that this wasn't how normal people did things. But I wasn't exactly taking advice from normal people anymore.

### A-Story meets B-Story

This wasn't my first time running. I had sprinted through my childhood, into early adulthood—mostly from myself. Growing up gay in the Midwest with a minister for a father wasn't exactly the runway to self-love and acceptance.

Our family could've been a melodramedy called *The Belasco Follies*: a no-nonsense preacher dad, a loving mother directing traffic with humor, and five kids not doing a great job of staying in their lane—except me, of course. In this mix were two gay boys headed in opposite directions—my brother popping out of Mom in a burst of Fruity Pebbles, wearing nothing but a tutu, belting "Somewhere Over the Rainbow," and me diving straight into the closet and locking the door behind me.

The tension between those worlds—faith and fabulousness—was quite a show. And as it turns out, Mom was teaching us how to love without limits, which, for me, took over half a century to land.

So after her passing, I wasn't running from anything but that house—I was searching.
For what? No clue. Maybe a lost marble or two.
Until Mom showed up.

Yes, my dear, dead one.
Not in an *I see dead people* kind of way—but in an *I'm talking with my dear, dead mom, and she's answering me* kind of way.

## Searching for Marbles, I Found Pearls

Some people inherit land, money, or maybe a timeshare in Boca. I got pearls—not the kind you wear around your neck, the kind that smack you upside the head and land squarely in your heart.

Mom had been dropping them my whole life—little nuggets of wisdom I dodged like bullets in *The Matrix*, like any "pretty" boy with an extended learning curve and a short attention span. Not too many of them landed. Not until she died.

On my road trip that spring after her death, pieces of Mom's life floated to the surface—softly rewriting the story I thought I understood about her, and about me. I started asking questions. Surprisingly, she began answering them with her pearls.

For the first time in over fifty years, I listened.
Those little nuggets weren't only filled with wisdom; they were a road map to a life I'd only dreamed of living. And they're a key reason this book exists.

## What This Book Is About

This book isn't just a road-trip story—though it was one hell of a ride.

It's about the bond between Mom and me, and how her love never stopped reaching me, even after she was gone.
It's also about family and faith and what happens when both collide in a glitter bomb. It's about how two gay sons of a preacher found their way to love—one in cha-cha heels, one in hiding—and how Mom's unconditional grace somehow kept us together, alive and out of prison.

It's about learning through loss, and how my "pretty" little mind finally caught up to the wisdom Mom lived every day.
Most of all, it's about how her unconditional love—and those posthumous pearls—helped me unlock the things I'd been chasing all along.

Once I finally started living what she taught me, my anxious, overthinking mind began to quiet, and lasting joy moved in. I now call that state of being **Peaceful Delight**, inspired by my mom. It's how she lived—and as I'm discovering, it's a beautiful place to reside.

This book is, in many ways, a long-overdue thank-you to Mom for a lifetime of love I didn't understand. Mom handed me the keys to more than a life worth living.
I found—**My Life Worth Loving.**

If that sounds like a place worth finding, scoot over—I'm driving.

## Disclaimer: It's All About Me

If you haven't figured it out, it's all about me. The book that is. It's told from my perspective, because that's the only one I've earned. I can't tell you what makes your life worth loving, and that isn't my goal, but I've a hunch that most of us are circling a few of the same basics.

I haven't figured it all out. I don't think that's possible—or even the point.

What I do have are receipts—what worked, what didn't, and the mess in between.

I can be irreverent, shameless, and wildly inappropriate—all beautiful gifts straight from Mom.

From Dad, I inherited the habit of talking *at* people, as if they were the congregation—or, in my case, anyone or anything willing to sit still.

Filters? I've got precisely one left, and it only kicks in around children. The rest of you? Good luck. Hopefully, you're not highly offendable.

And for the record, my younger brother Michael Todd once called me "the most self-absorbed human I know." His words.

That same night, he also labeled me "completely delusional."

He thought he was being helpful. I thought he was just jealous.

I was wrong.

He was right—as usual.

Me.

# Not Pretty—"Pretty"

Hello, my name is Jimmy, and I was born "pretty." Not the good kind. My kind of "pretty" comes with "air quotes," won't win a beauty contest—and is best served with a Public Service Announcement (PSA) and humble request:

PLEASE BE PATIENT. PLEASE BE KIND.

Come on, what kind of "pretty" comes with a set of air quotes and its own PSA? Mine.

Metaphorically, my "pretty" means a shortage of common sense and a lifetime for lessons to land. But physically? I wasn't pretty at all. I was painfully cute.

My chubby cheeks begged to be pinched, and my toe-head blonde hair practically demanded out-of-control fingers to pull through it. There was constant tugging and pulling. People, mostly women and girls, wouldn't shut up about my "impossibly long eyelashes" and gushed over my "bright-blue eyes," insisting they were "painted by the angels themselves." Ugh! I didn't get a moment's peace in public; it was Open Season on little Jimmy—"The Cutest Thing on Planet Earth." I hated it, the pinching, pulling, tugging, and gushing never stopped.

PEOPLE! STEP AWAY FROM THE PAINFULLY CUTE LITTLE BOY!

*He doesn't enjoy all the attention. Later in life, he'd wished he had a bit more pinching, pulling, tugging, and gushing, but for now—leave the kid alone!*

By age six or seven, I'd had enough. Armed with a pair of trusty kitchen scissors, I took matters into my own hands. Before Mom caught me, I had snipped off my eyelashes and hacked a large, crooked cut to my bangs. You can see evidence of this in the photo on page 4.

I thought I'd ended my torment, but I was wrong. My new asymmetrical bang and eyelash-less look made me even cuter in the eyes of my adoring, yet tormenting, public.

My suffering didn't end in childhood. While other kids endured awkward gangly phases, my unrelenting cuteness followed me into my teens.

Why did I have to be so cute?

I wanted to be handsome, like the guys who turned heads—and yes, one of those heads was mine. I wasn't sure why I was noticing them, but I couldn't stop.

Those kids fortunate enough to be born "not-so-cute" don't realize how good they had it—being perpetually cute is a tough hand to be dealt. Enough about me, I could go on all day about how cute I was—the struggle was real.

Let's meet the family.

# The Belasco Bunch

Me, at the epicenter. 1973

## Meet the Cast & Crew

Let me introduce you to the cast of characters who shaped me: my family. The Belasco Bunch consisted of my parents, five kids, and a dog named Spot. Well, Spot was with us for a while until Dad sent him away to "go live on a farm" because we didn't pick up his poop. Looking back, our "show" was far more entertaining than *The Brady Bunch*, my favorite TV sit-com in the early 1970s.

The kids in our family were the stars of the show, Dad was the Producer, and Mom was the Director. They set the stage for our performances. Dad was a preacher of an ultra-conservative religion, and Mom was his faithful but hilariously inappropriate wife. Mom had a lovely, twisted sense of humor, just dark enough to catch you off guard. Dad just didn't— twisted or otherwise.

FUN FACT: Michael Todd and I inherited our dark, twisted sense of humor from Mom. The only difference is that ours goes darker and deeper; we've yet to find the basement.

ANOTHER FUN FACT: The denomination we grew up in was so conservative that they thought the Baptists were "liberals" and going to hell. However, my parents were a bit less conservative, to put it mildly. If ultra-conservatism was the umbrella under which we grew up, our family was constantly soaking wet—I'm not even sure we knew there was an umbrella.

## A Quick Dive into the Belasco Kids

GERI ANN, the eldest, has lived her life as a *dramedy*—drama-induced comedy—and does so at a level of TEN. Her over-the-top responses to the everyday occurrences of her life aren't intentionally funny. Her propensity for over-dramatization and exaggeration turns even the tiniest events into hysterical spectacles. Geri Ann is delightful and fun to laugh with, and sometimes and often, at. She can turn nothingness into a hysterical storm with a name, and *Hurricane Geri Ann* sounds about right.

Geri Ann was my original playground protector in elementary school. If a bully dared to start something, she'd grab hold of their conveniently long 70s hair and repeatedly introduce their shins to her shoes.

JOHN DAVID, the second eldest, was my best friend and protector in high school. (Note that I needed a lot of protection.) Having a reputation as the "toughest kid in school," he didn't have to be the loudest in the room—often, it only took one harsh glance—or a swift punch to the face—whichever came first. As far as humor goes, he wasn't the one landing the punchline—that was my job—but he always laughed the loudest. His presence in my youth was both grounding and essential. He saved my life more than once. In high school, I once marched into his classroom, during class, and made him come out and talk to one of his friends who was threatening to beat me up—John set the guy straight. Nobody messed with John David or his smart-ass little brother, Jimmy.

Then there's me, JIMMY, the middle child, or epicenter as I like to think of it. I was the self-proclaimed Golden Child, the glue that held the family together, and of course, Mom's favorite. Enough about me—for now. I have the rest of the book for that.

After me came MICHAEL TODD, the "Rainbow-colored Black Sheep" and the family's creative genius. Oddly enough, despite being born five and a half years apart, we're like twins. We often share the same dreams, think the same thoughts, and even feel each other's physical and emotional pains. Once, I smashed my finger moving a refrigerator through a doorway. I was in Texas, he felt the pain, in the same finger at the same time, in New York.

His influence on my life has been profound—second only to Mom. There will be a greater focus on Michael Todd in this book than on my other siblings, because our stories intertwine so profoundly, and he has shaped me in ways that continue to define me. Plus, we're nearly twins. My other siblings, though lovingly a part of my life, play a less significant role in this story.

Finally, there's SUSAN. This poor kid grew up in the shadow of the three-ring circus, known as Michael Todd, who commanded all the air in the big tent. She may be one of the quietest, but she's the most intelligent and most level-headed. I once tried to argue with her, and her masterful logic muted my point instantaneously. I never tried again. She made my "I just felt like driving" moment possible and all the more enjoyable, as you'll learn.

## The Backdrop to The Belasco Follies?

The 1970s and 1980s framed *The Belasco Follies* in the suburbs of Detroit, where Yates Cider Mill, Coney Dogs, Vernor's pop, Louie's pizza, and Sander's Hot Fudge were the cure for everything, and still are.

## Dad, Discipline, and One Memorable Road Trip

Dad's discipline style fell somewhere between that of a Doberman and a fluffy bunny. There were threats of belts and spankings, sure—but most of the time, it was all bark, no belt. However, on one memorable road trip, when it was just Geri Ann, John David, and me, Dad hit Stage Four.

Dad had four stages of combustion, specially designed and reserved for road trips:

- Stage One: "Shut up! We're having fun! This is costing me a pretty penny!"
- Stage Two: "Don't make me use the Duct Tape." He used it often over our mouths. We made HELP! signs for passing cars, as they'd wave and laugh. You can't have fun like that anymore.
- Stage Three: "Don't make me stop this car and take off my belt!"
- Stage Four: Belt removal... and may God have mercy on us all.

We were mid-trip and mid-chaos going somewhere, not having an easy time "shutting up" and "having fun" on Dad's "pretty penny": hair pulling, shrieking, farting, and one of us pooped—possibly me. The car reeked of raw sewage and mayhem. After applying stages 1–3, Dad snapped. He yanked our olive-green 1970s wood-paneled station wagon off to the side of the road, its roof stacked high with luggage, secured with a blue tarp and bungee cords. I'm pretty sure we were the inspiration for the movie *National Lampoon's Vacation*. Here's what it looked like, sans the luggage on top.

Mom was screaming, "John! Please, don't!" as panic ensued in the back cargo area, where we kids spent our time tormenting everyone on board. With their feet, Geri Ann and John shoved me toward the rear door—where Dad was headed, belt in hand—as if I were the sacrificial lamb—which, apparently, I was.

The shape of the back door opening on a station wagon saved our lives that day. The low height-to-width ratio made it impossible to get a good swing. Dad, with wild-eyed rage, tried his damnedest, but nobody was getting hit but himself. What we couldn't see was that the buckle kept hitting his hand, and he started to bleed. I saw blood and started screaming as if I were being eaten by a bear.

We were going bananas, Dad's striking out, blood's flying everywhere, and Mom's got her foot on the bumper while pulling on his waistband and threatening divorce. Somehow, Mom's wiglet ended up on the front hood of the car—we thought we had hit a squirrel.

Ah, family vacations. We had joy, we had fun... and yes, we had seasons in the sun.

Nobody got spanked that day, except Dad. However, much to our delight, Stage Two was applied—Duct Tape. We silently cheered, HELP sign in hand—crisis over.

## This is Going to Hurt You More than it Hurts Me

As I remember it, aside from that road trip incident, Dad never punished us in anger. Let's just say, Dad wasn't as lucky growing up.

With us, there was always contemplation and conversation preceding the punishment phase, and always including this confusing statement: "This is going to hurt me more than it hurts you." I never understood that one; I think he had that backwards. Come to think of it, he did get that one right at least once—during that road trip.

## I Never Got the Belt

Whenever Dad pulled me into my parents' bedroom to receive my punishment, he would close the door so my giggling siblings couldn't see. He'd then whisper to me to yell when he smacked the two sides of the belt together to make a spanking sound. He did his thing, and I screamed like a murder was underway. A bit over-dramatic, but the cheers on the other side of the door told me our little charade had worked.

Years later, I asked Dad why he never spanked me. His reply?

"You were too cute. You'd look at me with those blue eyes filled with tears and say something like, 'Please, Daddy, don't hit me, I'm so little my feet don't touch the ground.' I just couldn't."

Cuteness, it turns out, is justice.

For all his theatrics, Dad wasn't abusive—to me, at least. He was tough, yes—he grew up on the streets of Boston—but around us, he mostly controlled his anger. John David was probably the exception; he did some pretty dumb stuff and always got caught. I watched what he did, then did the opposite, and stayed cute.

## Mom's Sweet Weapon of Mass Annoyance

Mom, on the other hand, never spanked us. Her go-to punishment was terrifying and straightforward: kneel in the corner and "think about what you've done—and what you're going to say to your father when he gets home." That alone could unravel your entire sense of self.

She didn't need volume or violence. Her real power? Quiet relentlessness and her perfectly manicured fingernails.

Every morning, she made it her mission to torment us awake. And I've confirmed with my siblings—none of us escaped her ritual. It was her morning performance, and we were each a captive audience.

She'd sit at the edge of the bed with that soft, "storytime" voice—adorable when you're five, enraging when you're fifteen. Then came the sequence:

With her perfectly manicured forefinger, she would slowly trace a line down my forehead, pry open one eyelid, take a trip up my nostrils, and circle my lips and chin, while saying:

"Forebender... eye-winker... nose-smeller... lip-kisser... chin-chopper..."

And then came tickles under my chin:

"Gilly, gilly, gilly..."

If I didn't bolt upright screaming, she moved on to Phase Two:

"Knock on the door," a forehead tap.

"Peek in the windows," an eyelid lift.

"Lift the hatch," a piggy-nose lift to open my lips.

"Walk right in," her fingers walked into my mouth.

Pretending to be still asleep was a rookie move.

By the end of high school, I was pleading:

"Mooooom! I'm nearly an adult! Stop already!"

Didn't matter.

Phase Three was coming:

"Are your happies awake?"

That meant a full-body tickle attack—under the arms, behind the knees, the works, like an adorable assassin in full makeup and false eyelashes.

I hated it.

I loved it.

Every morning.

What more could I say about Mom and Dad? Oh yeah, this...

## Shameless, Clueless, Highly Inappropriate—Just Right

If there's one story that sums up Mom and Dad, it's the infamous funeral when they unintentionally stole the show.

As blissfully oblivious as usual, Dad was walking down the long aisle to deliver the eulogy while crop-dusting a symphony of gaseous "toots" the entire way. When he reached the podium, he began the service as if nothing had happened.

The acoustics in the auditorium were spectacular—unfortunately so for Mom, who was sitting in the front row. She heard every sour note of Dad's one-man marching band as it traveled from the rear of the auditorium to the front. Also, unfortunately, Mom got tickled.

Mom was legendary for losing control of her bladder when she laughed too hard, and walking during one of these episodes was nearly impossible. Her usual coping mechanism was to stand with her legs crossed, like a pair of broken scissors. But in this situation, she had no choice but to leave as soon as possible before things went south. Herein lies the problem.

While trying to contain her laughter and her bladder, Mom attempted a cross-legged crab-walk-escape. But waves of giggles from her friends up the aisle made matters worse. Every step was an effort and a mess. Every few steps, she paused, shook with laughter, and then shuffled forward again, leaving a trail of tears, giggles, and let's say, more. Mom didn't make a clean exit.

Meanwhile, Dad carried on at the podium as if his highly inappropriate but faithful wife wasn't awkwardly laughing and peeing her way up the aisle during a funeral.

What I love most about this moment isn't just the absurdity, but also what it reveals about my parents. Mom, the preacher's wife, didn't, and couldn't, take life too seriously, even at a funeral. Most importantly, she felt no shame. She may have been embarrassed, but Mom was shameless—such an inspiration to us all.

As for Dad, I'm still unsure whether he was shameless, simply clueless, or maybe both. Either way, he was blissfully unfazed—such a trooper.

This story taught me two things:

Humor can carry you through even the darkest moments, and sometimes, the best response to life is to keep walking, laughing, and—if necessary—peeing your way up the aisle.

## Dad Accepted his Role

If that story wasn't a clue, Mom's humor usually fell just beyond the edge of good taste—one of her most remarkable qualities, in my opinion. We all enjoyed the same edge, well, except for dear, old Dad.

Dad was often the butt of jokes since humor wasn't one of his strengths. Once, when we had a sailboat, Dad was scrubbing the side of the boat while floating in a rubber dinghy. When he tried to climb onto the dock—several feet above the waterline—the dinghy kept sliding further under the dock, making the angle impossible. Each attempt only wedged him deeper into a network of big brown spiders and a wall of webs.

He called for help. We howled. The harder he tried, the madder he got. The madder he got, the more we laughed. Meanwhile, the dinghy started taking on water, and Dad kept sinking—better than any Carol Burnett skit I'd ever seen.

Threatening our lives got him nowhere, so he turned his sights on Mom, using his usual line when he was in a pickle: "Damn it, Jude! Do something!"

But one dock over, Mom was already cross-legged in hysterics, losing the battle with her bladder—the evidence spreading out beneath her onto the wood planks. By then, most of the marina had gathered for the show.

Eventually, Dad made it out—sweaty, red-faced, covered in spider bites, and wrapped in webs. We scattered like cockroaches, Mom included, though she was easy to track—she left a trail.

When we crept back about thirty minutes later, Dad was already busy with another project. Nothing was mentioned, as usual. Water under the bridge. Or, in this case, a sunken rubber dinghy under a dock.

## The UnOffendables

In recent years, I've realized something surprising:

It's damn near impossible to offend me. I can't remember the first time, let alone the last.

Recently, I asked someone what it felt like to be offended—because I genuinely couldn't remember. This also means I'm probably an offender without even knowing it. But it got me wondering where this came from.

Looking back, being "offended" just wasn't a thing in the Belasco household. I don't recall Mom or Dad ever using the word—or acting as if they were. We were a big and boisterous family; lots of digs, burns, slights, and playful insults. Boundaries? Yeah... nope. Nothing was off limits; the deeper the dig, the more we laughed, almost like it was a contest and a challenge.

Even with Dad usually landing on the back end of the joke, he'd just grumble a bit, move on, and never mention it again.

Mom set the tone; we never took ourselves too seriously—that dynamic shaped us. And because we knew how to laugh at ourselves first, nothing others might say could sting.

We were the UnOffendables.

## Sex Talk with Mom as an Adult?

Just before my parents moved in, I was sitting with Mom and one of my siblings (name withheld to protect the shameless), when they launched into a very graphic conversation about adult topics—sex, to be precise, using words and terms I would never utter in front of my mother. In fact, I never spoke about sex with Mom. And now I was hearing a full-on symposium on sex between my sibling and my mother—right there in the living room, as if they were swapping recipes.

Apparently, Mom was giving advice, as they openly delved deeper into the details. It was like I was watching a live version of "Hustler Forum" in Mom's living room. I was stunned by the terms Mom knew. I learned some new ones that night.

Once I regained my ability to speak, I finally asked, "Wait—is this how you two normally talk with each other?"

"Oh yes," they both said, "this is normal."

Was I offended? Nope. Somewhat horrified? Yep.

Entertained? Fully, against my will.

I grabbed the popcorn, blushed a lot, and watched the horror show.

## Those Are Nice Urns, Jim

Even after my parents moved in, that unoffendable energy remained. No one got offended by tone, politics, religion, or urns. Yes—urns.

When my folks moved in, I had two beautiful urns displayed on a shelf in their living room—each labeled with masking tape: "Mom" on one and "Dad" on the other. I told them, "You're living in my house now—my rules. If you can't control yourselves, these will be your new residences. Don't worry—I'll make all the arrangements."

Dark? Yes.

Funny? Mom laughed.

Dad said, "Those are nice urns, Jim."

### Mom!? Please, it's not even 8 AM!

And then this gem from when they lived with my husband and me:

The morning after my birthday, Mom walked into the kitchen beaming and giddy,

"So... did the birthday boy have great sex last night?"

I did a full spit-take and a complete 180, spraying half the kitchen with coffee on my way out.

She just giggled.

Was I offended? No.

Embarrassed? Hell yeah.

The most amusing part of this exchange was that she was genuinely interested, not just asking for shock value, this time.

### What Does This Say About My Parents?

They enjoyed the few freedoms they had, and they gave us ours:

The freedom to speak openly—even gay stuff, when we got older.

The freedom to be weird, wrong, or wildly inappropriate.

The courage to laugh at ourselves, because it's funny.

Perhaps laughing at myself early on helped build immunity, and shame doesn't stick because I don't carry it. When nothing is off-limits, and I've said worse things about myself, laughing harder than anyone else ever could, it seems nothing else stings.

Here's a fun example:

One day, around the age of eleven or twelve, just as I was entering puberty, a group of us kids were on the church bus heading somewhere. Behind me sat a couple of mean girls who were in the mood to torment a poor, unsuspecting, inept boy. Luckily for me and unfortunately for them, I was their target. They chose poorly.

They zeroed in on my forearms, where my long, blonde, well-kept arm hair caught their attention.

"GROSS! Look at Jimmy's arm hair! It's so long!" they shrieked, making sure every kid on the bus turned to gawk.

Now, let me be clear—I loved my arm hair, and still do.

Without missing a beat, I spun around, flashed them my most cherubic grin, and said, "You think that's bad? You should see the hair on my ass."

Remember, I was the preacher's kid; this was the early 1970s, and we were all about eleven or twelve. Appropriately so, this was highly inappropriate.

The bus erupted in laughter—but not at me. The girls were mortified; they took the hit here. Everyone was laughing at their reaction. I turned back around and sat there with a smug grin, knowing darn well that I didn't have any hair on my ass... yet. But now, they had to live with that visual.

This bus ride was probably when I first discovered this superpower of UnOffendability, though at the time it didn't have a name.

Over the years, Michael Todd and I took that spirit and ran with it—into the sparkly darkness. However, the credit belongs to Mom. Whether by design or by default, she raised at least two of us to be UnOffendable.

As for my other siblings, I'm unsure if they are still card-carrying UnOffendables.

No offense!

Dad & Mom

The Minister & His Wife

# Growing Up Gay with a Minister Dad

## Spotlights & Shadows

If you missed the not-so-subtle crumbs, two of us Belasco kids are gay. That's 40% of my parents' offspring—if you're into 6th-grade math—pretty high odds for a minister.

Growing up gay under the umbrella of an ultra-conservative religion looked very different for Michael Todd than it did for me. His umbrella was Miss Piggy pink, sequined and fringed; mine was Earth-toned camouflage.

As I mentioned in the Introduction—and it's worth repeating because the visual deserves an encore—Michael Todd popped out of Mom in a burst of Fruity Pebbles, wearing nothing but a tutu and belting "Somewhere Over the Rainbow." And that, my friends, was merely opening night for *The Gayest Show on Earth.* Try preaching a sermon to ultra-conservatives with *that* at the forefront of your mind—my poor parents.

From early on, he was unapologetically himself—and very, very gay, if there are levels. I, on the other hand, stayed hidden in a well-fortified closet, camouflaged by my Overachieving Golden Child persona—and my ability to manage what people knew about me with humor, a good story, a few failed attempts at sports, and "girlfriends." We'll get to all of that soon enough.

We both became masters at controlling the narrative: Michael boldly showed the world exactly who he was, and I masterfully drew attention to what I was great at, while also distancing myself from who I was.

Our shadows worked in opposite ways. In my youth, my bigger-than-life image cast a shadow that practically forced Michael Todd into the role of family misfit. And his defiance of expectations earned him nothing more than the title of the Black Sheep.

Unfortunately for Michael, I excelled academically, followed the rules, and, in the spirit of RuPaul, brought *charisma*, a dash of *uniqueness*, plenty of *nerve*, and *talent* to the game. On top of this, I "played well with others," as noted on every report card. I was a tough act to follow.

Years later, in high school, I found refuge in his shadow. He was hitting all the gay stereotypes of the time while I hid behind the magic curtain— "Look over there—that's what gay looks like. Nothing to see here." Not my proudest moment, but as I saw it then, I had everything to lose and nothing to gain by showing my glittery side.

And where were my parents in all this? Well, I gave them nothing to deal with other than keeping up with good report cards. Mom—ever the peacemaker—tried to keep the family buttoned up, smoothing feathers while quietly loving us all the same.

Dad seemed more puzzled than angry, as if Michael Todd's sparkly way of being was just a phase, until it wasn't. By the time Dad realized it wasn't going away, it had become unstoppable.

Our paths to self-acceptance couldn't have been more different. Michael Todd lived out, loud, and proud. I chose to read a nice book inside, in the closet. I thought I'd outsmarted the whole system—until *someone* imploded my closet, exposing me to the world. But that's a fun little tale that we'll go over in detail later.

Speaking of Karma
(Who was speaking of karma?)

Nothing in life is black and white, but our ultra-conservative world then insisted otherwise. Rules were rigid, and the consequences were harsh. Excommunication—being voted off the island—was one of them.

You or your family could be excommunicated for:

- **Divorce**
- **Remarriage**
- **Sex outside of marriage**
- **Being gay**

Unfortunately for my parents, they hit the unholy jackpot—every single one of these offenses got checked off by their children, each of us with multiple infractions.

My faithful parents—a minister and his wife—ended up with:

- **Two daughters, and five sons-in-law** (unpack that one)
- **One frisky "girl-crazy" boy** (biblically speaking)
- **Two gay sons** (if one wasn't enough)

If you're counting qualifying offenses against the short list provided at the top, the sheer numbers at this point would be impossible; my parents might've qualified for a good old-fashioned stoning.

For heaven-sake! What did my poor parents do to earn this?

Who were they in their past lives—Bonnie and Clyde?

The point is that they turned out to be the opposite in this lifetime. My parents were loving, kind, and faithful people. But like old Bonnie and Clyde, they had the odds stacked against them—they didn't have a running chance.

Oh, the stress we put our poor parents through.

## A Temporary Absence

In the middle stretch of my story, you may notice that my family fades into the background. It isn't a rift—it's timing. In college, closeted, I kept visits minimal and short to dodge the "girlfriend?" questions. Later, in Dallas, I buried myself in work and saw everyone maybe once a year. The details of my family from those decades are fuzzy because I wasn't around. If they feel absent, that's on me. Don't worry—my life converges again with my parents, though not in ways I could have imagined.

Now that I've set the stage, I believe "the greatest day of my life" is the perfect place to begin my story,

# "My Special Day!"

## The Day That Made Me, Me

Before me was a sea of stripes, bright colors, bold patterns—even polka dots—just like the clothes I'd seen on TV and dreamed of wearing someday. And that day was today—the greatest day of my life.

As I stood there at the edge of the Boys' Department, I was already fast-forwarding to the first day of school in my mind. There I was, strutting into the building in one of my groovy new outfits, flashing the peace sign as the crowd of students parted in awe. The paparazzi were snapping photos. Reporters were crying out my name. The principal fainted from the sheer beauty of it all.

My Special Day—the day that would forever shape the story of one fabulous little boy. The kind of day people write songs about, in fact, I did. Here's the one I wrote (to the tune of the Brady Bunch theme song):

> Here's the story... of a boy named Jimmy.
> I had to wear my older brother's hand-me-downs.
> With patches on the knees and stretched out elbows,
> And grass stains made me frown.
>
> Till the one day when us kids were given new clothes,
> And I knew that it was much more than a hunch,
> That these new clothes would change my life forever.
> That's the way I'll look just like the Brady Bunch!
>
> My Special Day!
> My Special Day!
> That's the day... I'll look like the Brady Bunch!

## Flashback: How We Got Here

It was the summer of 1971, just before school started, and the Belasco kids had just scored big. Thanks to a generous sponsor—churchgoers who owned Dearborn's most fashionable department store—we were each gifted two brand-new, head-to-toe outfits.

And not just any store: Muirhead's—the crème de la crème of Midwestern retail. The kind of place where stylish ladies lunched, fashionable women came to buy status, and mothers brought their children to spoil them. The entire basement was a luxury Toy Department. It was awesome. Each story of the building showcased the latest fashions, from children's wear to haute couture.

This amazing day would be my first time wearing clothes that hadn't already lived a full life on my older brother John David's body—knee patches, grass stains, and stretched-out elbows included. Nope. The clothing before me that day was glorious, untouched, groovy magnificence. I was on the verge of attaining a whole new level of status in life.

Mom knew better than to take more than one child at a time. I wore her down with the kind of persistent enthusiasm only a seven-year-old with a fashion dream can conjure—I badgered her incessantly. She eventually gave in and took me first. Obviously, I deserved it most.

On the morning of My Special Day, I was up before dawn, dressed, with the car keys in hand, before she was even awake. Guess who woke her up? When she entered the kitchen, where I was impatiently waiting, she laughed as I handed her the keys, and we were off.

"No time for coffee, Mom! They're expecting me. I CANNOT be late!"

We arrived exactly thirty-one minutes early. "Right on time, Mom!" Mom, in her beautiful and bold black-and-white houndstooth dress suit, looked as elegant as ever. I was proud she was my mom. On the other hand, I pulled together the best ragamuffin outfit I had and hoped nobody noticed. Here's a picture from a few years earlier, of her in that dress. That's me being painfully cute on Dad's lap.

At the entrance, a sharply dressed woman greeted us, whom we'll call Betty. Just past the glass doors, a welcome sign read:

Today's Special Guest: Jimmy Belasco

My chest puffed up. I knew exactly where I was headed and strutted in like a pint-sized peacock on a mission—Muirhead's Boys' Department. Or as I saw it, the Land of Fabulousness, a sacred place that lived in my head.

Betty dropped us off at the entrance and said a saleswoman would be with us shortly.

FUN FACT: In the early 1970s, female sales staff were still referred to as "saleswomen." They weren't recognized as "people" until years later, when they became *salespeople*—another leap forward in Women's Rights.

That's where we pick back up the story, as I stood there frozen at the edge of the Boys' Department, fantasizing about my first day of school.

The clothes—my clothes—were all there. Bright colors, bold stripes, even polka dots! It all screamed, "Bobby and Greg Brady realness." I wasn't a fan of Peter Brady's fashion sense, so he wasn't on my mind.

I was already planning my photoshoot when I heard two words from the world outside of my head that shattered the fantasy.

"...wrong section."

My head spun around like Linda Blair's in *The Exorcist*.

Standing behind Mom was a tall, rigid saleswoman—we'll call her Jane. Think Jane Hathaway from *The Beverly Hillbillies*, only more judgmental and less amused. Jane's disapproval hit like a sniper. Her eyes scanned me up and down like I was an inventory mistake.

"WRONG SECTION?" I blurted, hands on hips. I pointed to the sign above us. "BOYS' DEPARTMENT!" I pointed to myself. "I'm a BOY!"

Jane nodded, unbothered. "Ma'am, I can see your son is a boy..." she said, speaking about me—but never to me, and looking at me, but right through me. That was puzzling. Then she continued,

"As I stated, Ma'am, you and your son are in the wrong section; this is the Slim Boys' section."

"SLIM? As in Slim Jims? I eat those all the time." I'd only ever heard that word in reference to Slim Jims Sausage Sticks, and I ate those by the handful. "What do Slim Jims have to do with this?" I demanded.

I glanced at Mom, confused. I wasn't tracking irony yet—I was seven.

Mom stood silent, either entertained or horrified by the situation; I couldn't tell. That was perfectly fine with me—I'd been handling adult situations like this my whole life.

But Jane wasn't done with me yet. With a hushed tone that somehow made it louder, she dropped the bomb—more specifically, the H-Bomb:

"Your son is... (as she looked over each of her shoulders to see if the coast was clear)... **HUSKY**."

"HUSKY? Our neighbor's dog is a HUSKY! I'm a BOY—not a dog!"

I protested the whole way as they dragged me, toes down and in full-body-limp-mode, away from the clothing I adored. I didn't know where they were taking me, but I knew it wasn't good, so I was not going to be a willing participant. My feet—and my will to live—tried their best to stay in the Land of Fabulousness, but Jane was not going to have that happen on her watch.

They plopped me in a heap in front of a colorless rack of clothing, where everything was beige. The shirts. The pants. Even the jeans weren't blue—they were beige jeans. Above this rack of sadness hung a sign in big, fat, chunky letters that read:

**HUSKY BOYS**

That's when it hit me: I was too plump to wear the clothes I loved. That sign might as well have read: DOUGH BOYS.

As it turns out, there's an entire line of clothing made specifically for chubby little boys who prefer bread and butter to exercise. What sick-minded person puts dough-colored clothes on kids who already look like rising dough?

And just in case the shame wasn't clear enough, each pair of beige jeans came with a giant **HUSKY** tag—on the outside of the waistband, in two-inch letters. All-beige wear for chubby boys was bad enough, as it made it easier for the bullies to spot us; we nearly glowed in the dark, but the huge **HUSKY** authentication tag verified they had caught one. Beige was not a color; it was a shaming device. "Yoo-hoo! Fatty over here!"

My seven-year-old dreams dissolved into a beige nightmare that day. I didn't just walk out with two new, entirely beige outfits. I walked out with a brand-new belief:

My body was wrong.

It was the day I learned shame had a size.

And apparently, its name was **HUSKY**.

The painfully cute photo of me on page 4 is from this time period, possibly the year before, and it doesn't appear that I am chubby.

Was I too fat for the groovy clothes, or did we catch Jane on a bad day? Was she trying to steer us away from the expensive clothes to save the owners a few bucks?

Who knows, but it affected me; I grew up hating my body into adulthood.

There seem to be some lessons I learned from this—we'll reflect on them later down the road when I'm an adult.

Let's continue with my childhood...

As I'd soon discover, I had a natural talent that might help me survive this direct hit to my psyche.

# My Weekly Gig at the Widow's Peak

## How to Kill It at Church and Not Go to Jail

One fateful Sunday morning, near the age of the HUSKY incident, before the church service started, I found myself standing in the pew in front of the Widow's Peak (the section where the ladies without husbands sat), staring at them, and they at me. It was awkward. I didn't quite know why I ended up standing there, but when I eventually opened my mouth, the funny fell out. I was an instant hit!

As an avid over-sharer, my stories revolved around my family's "hidden" inner workings, some might call "family secrets"—arguably the most inappropriate fodder for a preacher's kid to hand over to the church gossip mill. Words popped into my head, skipped right past the processors of appropriateness, and rolled out of my mouth.

Editing? Filtering? That's for quitters. These weren't concepts I was familiar with at seven—or even today, for that matter.

My material was spontaneous and wildly inappropriate, which, in our ultra-conservative world, made it all the more deliciously entertaining. I loved every second of it, and seemingly, so did my, quite literally, captive audience at the Widow's Peak.

I'm unsure whether it was my words, impossibly long eyelashes, or my adorable delivery, but I thoroughly killed it at the Widow's Peak every time. I'm pretty sure I made a few of them pee a little. But wasn't that to be expected? Depends.

Making people laugh, especially when they probably shouldn't be laughing, brought me more joy than anything else in my young life. Sunday mornings quickly became my favorite time of the week, for all the "wrong," but oh, so right, reasons.

For most of my youth, until I went off to college, the Widow's Peak became my standing weekly gig. I'd arrive without a plan, step onto my metaphorical stage, and open my mouth. I never knew what I'd say until I said it, but the funny always spilled out, and the laughs kept coming.

## And Today?

That's as true today as it was then. If I have an audience, the humor flows uncontrollably. Although I cannot recall specific examples from my childhood performances, I can assure you that this spontaneous combustion was happening then, just as it is now.

Here's a perfect, more recent example:

One day, I stopped by Maggie's house unannounced. Maggie is one of my best friends and my ex's mother. We have a long history of playful banter, though this exchange surprised us both.

She answered the door and greeted me in her sweet country drawl, "Had I known you were coming, I'd have put on a bra!" What came from my lips next had never run through my mind before this moment; it just popped out, without pause.

"Oh, I just thought you were wearing open-toed shoes."

We both froze in awe of the words that had fallen out of my mouth. As the visual sank in, Maggie chuckled. "Get your ass in here... and don't be steppin' on my boobs." Touché, Maggie! Touché!

Humor and a good story, as I soon discovered, allowed me to control the room and direct people's attention to and from where I wanted—to my strengths and away from insecurities and soon-to-be rainbow-colored secrets.

# Lost in My Own Fabulousness

## Just Me, Myself, and... Oh, Right, Other People

Have you ever heard of the Self-Attention Surplus Stage, one of the stages in the SASS gauging system?

No? That's because I invented it for myself. It gauges my self-awareness, or self-absorption levels, at any given time. I didn't create the behaviors—I just perfected them and gave them a name. I was full of SASS.

SASS has four stages that roughly map my life—from childhood to the present. The arc spans from the full-blown Self-Absorption Syndrome Stage to the Self-Awareness Surplus Stage. We'll get to the inner workings of my SASS Meter shortly.

Mine started early, with basic skills forged from two things I didn't know how to manage: a husky body I hated and a colorful secret I had to hide. Managing what the world knew about me required a great deal of self-attention and focus.

Luckily, I backed into a series of things that became a kind of Wilderness Survival Kit. Learning early that "good deeds" garner a lot of attention, I became a "good boy." As I learned about my sense of humor and ability to tell great stories, this combination kept attention where I wanted it. Basically, I learned to dazzle them with my brilliance. And dazzle, I did.

Anything I found I was good at, I focused on and excelled. My first focus was on my school work; it came easily to me, so I became an excellent student. Then I learned that I had a good singing voice, so I became an excellent singer. Then I learned about the power of fashion. Fashion changed my image and commanded positive attention.

I entered my freshman year of high school, looking like Farrah Fawcett's little brother, sporting fade-tinted glasses and my hair parted in the middle, feathered. Shortly after this phase, the Urban Cowboy fad emerged, and my cowboy hat featured a majestic, feathered spray on the front. Earlier that decade, bell-bottom pants, polyester shirts in wild patterns, and platform shoes made me feel taller, shinier, more important than the husky, closeted boy underneath.

I started working at fourteen to cover my *needs* and fulfill my *wants*. By fifteen, before I had my driver's license, I had a brand-new 1979 cinnamon-brown Camaro, with a backup 1967 Dodge Dart, waiting for the day I was sixteen. Just because, why not?

When the preppy look took over in the 1980s, I traded my urban cowboy hat for a Polo, and it felt like slipping into a uniform I was born to wear.

Deck shoes, khakis, woven cotton belts, buttoned-down oxfords, with a minimum of two polo shirts underneath, with the collars flipped up.

I wore oversized horn-rimmed glasses and had my hair highlighted to a brassy blonde using a spray-on product called Sun-In.

In a Detroit-area youth chorus started by Dad's church, I sang my way up to a key male soloist, and held that spot until college. Once in college, I did the same thing again, and more: choir solos, baritone in a six-part a cappella touring group, and two years in a row as co-host of their big spring singing extravaganza. They called me Jimbo—so preppy.

In general, if I was going to do something, I had to be the best; otherwise, I didn't bother. Everything about me was image and success-driven—controlling where people looked, what they noticed, and what stayed hidden. Now I see it, but back then, I wasn't fully aware of it.

Here's the strange part—as insufferable as all this sounds, even to me right now, people seemed to like me anyway. Maybe the cute factor was still working in my favor. Or maybe nobody actually noticed any of it, and it was all just in my head. Whatever it was, it worked.

Back then, I wasn't analyzing it. I was doing it, and somehow it was protecting me. I didn't think of it as survival because, through it all, I was thriving.

Looking back now with my master-level overthinker's degree, I can see more clearly that my SASS contained the skills I needed, and luckily, they were likable, and somehow so was I. Back then, my SASS skills saved me; later, they advanced to new levels and nearly destroyed me.

When I was a kid and a young man, my SASS was a Level 2. In adulthood, I fluctuated between Levels 2 and 4. These days, somewhere near Level 1.

What are all these levels, you ask?

Next page. It's my SASS Meter, which I created to help me track my Self-Attention Surplus Stage day to day.

# Jimmy's SASS Meter

## LEVEL 1 – **Self-AWARENESS Surplus Stage** (SASS-1)

- Noticing other people exist and actually connecting with them.
- Listening more, talking (slightly) less. It is possible.
- Your love, likability, and fabulousness factors are off the charts.
- Showing patience & kindness to self and others—finally.
- Feels suspiciously like maturity, but let's not call it that.

## LEVEL 2 – **Self-ATTENTION Surplus Stage** (SASS-2)

- The spotlight is firmly on you—it's portable.
- Your self-controlled good lighting shows only your best angles.
- Hair, cars, clothes, social status: the fabulousness factor is high.
- Knowing others exist—mostly as your audience.
- "Delightfully tolerable"—somehow, people still like you.

## LEVEL 3 – **Self-ABSORPTION Surplus Stage** (SASS-3)

- Absorption Mode: image, success, and status are your oxygen.
- Your likability & fabulousness factors tank—you're barely tolerable.
- You're exhausting. To everyone—including yourself.
- You're too busy performing to notice any of this.
- Warning: Prolonged exposure may lead to Dark Periods and a diet of 99-cent double cheeseburgers and colas.

## LEVEL 4 – **Self-ABSORPTION "Syndrome" Stage** (SASS-4)

- You've crossed from "Surplus" into a self-imposed "Syndrome."
- You're just a jerk. Some might even call you an "Ass!"
- It's time for an intervention.
- Rescue a dog, or 13 dogs, and a cat named George. They'll place bets on who will outlive you. If you're lucky, you might learn to *love like a dog* before they win the bet.

To give you an idea of how I use the chart, I'll sprinkle a few ratings throughout the book.

A "quick reference" copy is available at the end of this book.

# Ultra-Conservative-ish

### "Ish" Happens

My ultra-conservative upbringing eventually played a pivotal role in shaping the relationship between my parents and me later in life, though perhaps not in the way you'd expect. As this tale unfolds, that connection will come full circle. Don't worry, I will point it out when we get there. For now, let's say that growing up in an ultra-conservative religion was both a defining experience and a perplexing one.

And this is where the "ish" comes into play. Within that tiny "ish," my world came alive and shaped me into the person I am today. I flourished within the inherent "ishness" within my ultra-conservative world.

I pause to clarify something, especially for my childhood church friends reading this. I loved my upbringing—not necessarily because of the religion itself, mind you, but because of the people. The people were the heart of my childhood. They filled my life with love and some of my most joy-filled memories. Many of these people are still my closest friends.

So, let's be clear: It wasn't the people who confused me. It was some of the church's rules.

Please don't take anything I say too seriously—I'm not.

## Top Three List of No-Nos

Trust me, these rules all tie into the beauty of this story; it will become apparent later.

Without further ado, I present the Top Three No-Nos of the religion of my youth, as I see them.

### Rule #1: NO DRINKING ALCOHOL—EVER!

This one's as simple and sweet as the grapes that make wine. You know, the stuff Jesus made. You may be aware of His signature vintage blend, "Miracle #1."

That's what puzzled me. If it was righteous enough for Jesus to create, miraculously no less, and serve at all His dinner parties, why was it such a big No-No for us, His faithful followers?

### Rule #2: NO DANCING—EVER!

Now, this one's a Turducken of Tales—a mystery stuffed with contradictions and wrapped in absurdity. If you're unfamiliar, a Turducken involves a duck, a chicken, and a turkey, all stuffed together into a culinary monstrosity. Puzzling? Yes. Delicious? Surprisingly so— just like this story.

Here's the deal: the church strictly forbade dancing. We weren't allowed to go to school dances, which was fine with me since I wasn't interested in dancing with girls. And married couples? Forget it. Dancing was off-limits there as well.

It is now where the story turns Turducken. A high school friend of mine started attending church with me, and soon after, so did his parents. This form of outreach was encouraged—bringing lost sheep to the fold—but it was my first and final attempt. My friend's parents were *ballroom dancers* and wanted to perform at our church's talent show. ACCESS DENIED! They left the church without an explanation, and my friend was no longer allowed to hang out with me.

The church lost some sheep that day, and I lost a friend.

Now for the mysterious twist. On the first Monday of every month, our ultra-conservative area churches rented a skating rink—and my dad, the minister, was the ringleader. We strapped four wheels to our feet and danced the night away under disco balls to songs like "Shake Your Booty," "Ring My Bell," and "Let's Get It On." Of course, not a soul mentioned the word dancing—it was *skating*, and somehow dancing on skates was righteous.

My parents were the best dancers—or *skaters* in the place. They boogied across the rink with moves that could've landed them as background dancers in the movie *Saturday Night Fever*. Then there were the slow songs, where their graceful gliding looked suspiciously like *ballroom dancing* to me. And yet, somehow, this wasn't "dancing-on-wheels." Turducken, indeed.

Maybe my friend's parents should have offered to put some wheels on their feet—Ballroom Skating could've become a thing at our church. I would have kept a friend, and the church might have gained some sheep.

Each night at the rink, they held a few "Couples Only" skates, and my parents would head out and give a Gold Medal performance. Oddly enough, Dad would also skate with women besides my mom, and no one blinked an eye! Not even me. It's just what we did on the first Monday of every month. Even the Elders and Deacons of the church and their families attended these Roller-Dance-Capades.

I'm so happy for whatever mind-warp was occurring, because some of my fondest memories happened in that place; you'll hear about a very special one in a few pages. I applaud my dad for having the absolute balls to pull off The Greatest Magic Trick on Earth by making "dancing-on-wheels" somehow righteous in the eyes of our ultra-conservative community.

Recently, I asked Dad what he was thinking when he introduced roller-dancing to a bunch of ultra-conservatives. His answer? "Well, Jim, the Bible doesn't mention *skating*, so I figured it was fine." Atta boy, Dad! Grab that "ish" by the tail and swing on it!

Now, let's get down to a subject near and dear to my heart.

## Rule #3: NO HOMOSEXUALING—EVER!

Ah, the big one. Homosexuality wasn't just a sin in our religion; it was the Unmentionable Sin, as the word was only spoken in hushed tones as if it were a mental illness. Sadly, up until the early 70s, homosexuality was thought of as a mental illness in the world of psychology.

I thought, *Thank goodness I'm not one of them!* Isn't that sweet?

### "Tendencies"

For those who couldn't commit, or weren't willing to admit, to being "full-time" homosexuals, the Wonderful World of Words (WWoW) offered a consolation label: *Homosexual Tendencies.*

It was the part-time option for those people who just *tended to* splash around in the big gay pool without cannonballing in. "It's just a phase," they'd say, "Little Johnny's just got tendencies. It'll wear off soon enough." This loophole word allowed families to keep their members with "questionable leanings" safe from excommunication.

I'll admit I found comfort and refuge in this term a time or two in college. It allowed me to avoid full disclosure, even to myself.

On the other hand, if you were a *known homosexual,* they would say, "He's a *confirmed bachelor.*" You never wanted to be "confirmed"—especially when we had "tendencies" at our disposal.

### The Perfect Sin

According to some, *drinking, dancing,* and *homosexualing* are the unholy trinity of sins—any one of these could act as the "gateway drug" leading to the other two. Combine all three, and you have:

The Perfect Sin.

As a little boy with budding, unsolicited crushes on guys, this concept terrified me. As the shameless man standing before you now, The Perfect Sin sounds like the perfect evening out—and a damn good name for a dance club.

Let's recap the Top Three Rules, shall we:

- **No Drinking**—unless Jesus Himself makes you a drink.
- **No Dancing**—unless it's on wheels.
- **No Homosexualing**—unless it's just "tendencies."

Ultra-conservative-ish!

That's fine with me; it all hangs on that "ish!"

Me, sporting an Urban Cowboy shirt & Dorothy Hamill haircut, 1975.

# My Coming Out—Party of One!

### Guess Who Had One?

Telling this story takes courage. Either that, or I have no shame and really like oversharing. Here it goes.

Have you ever heard of debutante balls? These are glamorous events where young women, mainly in the South, are formally "presented to society," also known as Coming Out Parties.

Well, guess who had a Coming Out Party?

Have you ever seen that moment when a little boy realizes he's not like the other boys?

Hold on, this one's fun.

### Picture it. A Roller Rink in a Detroit Suburb. 1975.

An eleven-year-old me, an adorably chubby prepubescent boy, was skating my heart out—thinking I was Dorothy Hamill. I even had the haircut. I was serving professional skater realness. Or at least, that's how it looked in my head. It only gets better.

Somehow, this eleven-year-old boy acquired a pink, poofy-sleeved pirate shirt that paired nicely with his bell-bottoms. Yes, you read that right. Those poofy pink sleeves flounced and fluttered with every graceful movement of my fleshy arms, catching the breeze like tiny flags of freedom. If the song from *West Side Story*, "I Feel Pretty," wasn't playing in my head, it absolutely should've been.

I felt so pretty! (the good kind)

I skated with the confidence of a seasoned performer, lost in my fabulousness. I wasn't just skating; I was letting them have it, all of it, on that floor—the performance of a lifetime. My inner diva had fully taken over my body. The rink was my stage, and I was the star. Every eye in the place was on me...

[screech—music halts]

But that's not what happened. Well, all of *it* happened except the very last part—not one soul noticed! All that beauty, all that grace—wasted. On everyone!

There was no applause, no ovations, and no "10's across the board!"— nothing! And oddly enough, I didn't notice any side-eyed glances, no disapproving shakes of the head—simply no reaction at all.

Even after that night, there was no mention of it, no hushed discussions, and trust me, I had eyes and ears all over that church. I was the preacher's kid and had my finger firmly on the pulse of church gossip; I contributed my fair share and controlled most of its content. I was the mayor of that little village, and in my gang were the daughters of the Elders and Deacons. I would've been the first to know if anyone had commented on my poofy, pink-sleeved moment.

## Count My Lucky Stars!

Yes, there was a side of me that was highly disappointed that nobody noticed, and I'm not sure how they missed it! But thankfully, they did. Maybe I blinded them with my brilliance—yet again... literally.

Who knows, but count my lucky stars! That was the absolutely wrong crowd with which to share my "coming-out confirmation" moment.

One thing's for sure: that pink non-gender-specific blouse had magical powers. For a young, budding gay boy, I couldn't wear pink poofy sleeves, bell-bottoms, sporting a Dorothy Hamill haircut, and roller skates while "Love to Love You Baby" plays... and not feel something. That evening, a door unlocked deep within me. My true self came out to play.

*I can never let that happen again!*

## Not Like the Other Boys!

That night sealed the deal on the guy crushes I'd been wrestling with. I didn't fully understand it, but I knew, at age eleven, I was not like the other boys.

I was terrified. After hearing the hushed condemnation throughout my youth in our circles, I had to keep this locked deep inside—nobody could ever find out.

It was no longer just my body that betrayed me; now my mind, my emotions, and every fiber of my being were waging war against everything I was taught to believe.

*My insides are all wrong... I must guard this with my life!*

So, this cute, pubescent little boy built a well-fortified, pink-lined closet to keep my darkest secrets safe. That closet became my sanctuary and my prison for the next decade.

And the pink blouse with flouncy sleeves? I never saw it again. Maybe someone burned it to protect me. Maybe my younger brother stole it to perform some Voodoo magic on me years later. I have my suspicions, but we may never know.

Speaking of flouncy blouses...

# Maybe I Should've Just Been a Caterer

## No Tendencies Here

Here's the hitch for my dear, lovely parents back in the 80s: two of their five kids were gay—no part-time tendencies. Jimmy was in hiding; Michael Todd was not. Either way, not ideal for a preacher in an ultra-conservative church. The unwritten rule was simple:

*"If you can't control your kids, how can you lead your sheep?"*

Had the congregation known there were two of us, they may have forced Dad to trade in his "preacher's cloth" for an apron.

You see, earlier in life, Dad was a pastry chef and worked in several commercial kitchens. On the side, throughout our childhood, he continued to work as a caterer to make ends meet. Amid Michael Todd's mayhem, on more than one occasion, I heard Dad mutter:

"Oh, Jeez! Maybe I should've just been a caterer."

## Miss Piggy, A Tutu & Pirouettes

Luckily for my parents, my pink closet was lined with reinforced brilliance and protected by my willingness to conform, as I sought to survive in a world that was telling me everything I knew about myself was wrong.

Michael Todd could not hide his rainbow—there wasn't a closet big enough. By five, he was pirouetting through our backyard in a tutu, composing eulogy-worthy poetry, and designing beaded wedding gowns for my sister's Miss Piggy doll. He flitted, floated, pranced, and danced.

Unfortunately for my parents, our house was on the front corner of the church property. Our backyard was surrounded on two sides by the church building, complete with a whole wall of windows along the length of our yard that looked out onto Michael Todd's main stage. So, his outdoor ballets weren't private performances—they were matinee shows for anyone interested—or those gathering evidence.

At first, Michael Todd's childhood sparkle was endearing to the church folk. But as he got older, their concerns morphed into a full-blown "crisis of masculinity." There was an unwritten expectation that Dad needed to "fix" this situation if he wanted to remain a minister.

## Mission Impossible—Here "We" Come!

Dad enrolled Michael Todd in the Scouts and drafted me, kicking and screaming, to be a Junior Scout Leader. My assigned mission: KEEP THE KID ALIVE. Their mission? A hope that camping in the wilderness and Snipe hunts would engage his masculinity.

I now had yet one more identity to hide in my closet from my high school friends, which included a red beret, neckerchief, too-tight shorts, and tall, itchy socks. This Scouting situation lasted my entire senior year in high school—an awful long time to keep a Junior Scout Leader uniform a secret. And, of course, I did.

I should have received a wilderness badge for that.

As far as my Scouting mission? I kept him alive. Their mission? Failure: Masculinity levels not achieved.

Just as I predicted.

Blood was in the water, and the sharks were circling—the "powers to be" recommended more drastic measures. Mom told me years later that they felt their hands were tied and that it was not what they felt was right. But the course of action was laid out for them.

They complied.

What follows is not something I take lightly; however, mocking its absurdity is how I manage the true horrors. None of this is funny. It was all too real—and all too wrong. These types of programs destroyed people's lives and ended many of them. Though it might sound like it, I don't take any of this lightly.

## Conversion Anyone?

Attempt #1. The first conversion attempt on his life, the organization had some horrible acronym for a name—something like Camp C.H.A.N.G.E. Conversioning Homosexuals And Normalizing Gender Expression, or something equally ridiculous. What's truly ridiculous is that anyone could believe you can change who you're naturally attracted to. Have you ever tried? I tried throughout my entire youth through college. It didn't work, but I suppose you're aware of that by now.

They gave the old "Pray-the-Gay-Away" routine their best shot, along with other useless tactics, but they couldn't "c.h.a.n.g.e." him. The Camp Director happily handed Michael Todd back to my parents.

"Your son was not a willing participant in his conversion. I don't believe there is any hope of his recovery."

Next up, Attempt #2, a true horror story. A so-called "counselor"—let's call him: Creep-o-the-Clownselor. This truly disturbed man suggested that Michael Todd, *in his early teens*, mind you, should *sleep with several women... under his supervision.*

Who gave this individual the authority to be around children? I hope he went to prison.

Luckily, before any of the craziness happened, while listening to his "therapy" plan, Michael Todd responded like any self-respecting teen icon: he flipped him off and walked out.

To my parents' horror—and their admitted fault—they hadn't checked out what kind of "therapy" was being offered until Michael Todd alerted them. Years later, Mom told me that not checking into this guy's therapy ahead of time was her greatest regret.

Attempt #3, and final attempt, my parents took charge of this process and chose a Christian counselor they'd known for years and trusted, who did not perform conversion therapies. After working with Michael Todd for some time, she gave them her assessment:

"Your son is homosexual. That's not something to *fix*—it's simply who he is. You cannot change his natural attraction, just as you cannot change your own. You can love him as he is, or you may lose him trying to force him into a life that isn't his."

Brava, Mrs. 1980s Christian Counselor. Take a bow.

My parents chose the LOVE option. But by then, the damage was done.

## Michael Todd Shared his Story

Conversations with Michael Todd in recent times are the basis for the above information, though I intentionally omitted or changed some details. I hadn't known the full story until then. When I read this to him, he thanked me.

"I wouldn't have been able to tell the story through the pain. Mine would have been a much darker, angrier story. You handled it beautifully. Thank you!"

"Honestly, Jim, I felt abandoned by the very people who should have protected me. This abandonment crushed me. I had no one to turn to, and the person I turned to at church—who said they were my friend and on my side—turned on me and started this whole ball rolling. It wasn't Mom and Dad, but I was furious with them for letting this happen to me.

When they finally stopped the process after the last one, which thankfully opened their eyes, I couldn't accept their love. I was pissed. I was going to let the world know who I was.

I knew it wasn't going to be pretty—it was going to be fabulous!

You know what was pulsing through my veins, Jim?

*Gay? They want to see Gay? I'll show them GAY!*"

# The Gayest Show on Earth!

The New & Improved Michael Todd, 1986.

Michael Todd (17 years old). A night out in Chicago.
About 3 years into his "show," 1987.

Michael Todd became the Ringmaster of what I now lovingly refer to as:

**Michael Todd and his Midnight Circus—The Gayest Show on Earth!**

A gender-fluid spectacle staged in our backyard and anywhere else he could pitch a tent. Or as circus folk call it, The Big Top.

Michael Todd was the whole damn show: tent, spotlight, costumes, trapeze artist, Ringmaster, and Boss Clown. It was bold, brilliant, and terrifying. Even death-defying!

"I'm Coming Out" (Diana Ross) blasted the radio—and that he did.

His aesthetic? A Gender Bender Blender, by Gay-Co, chock full of Boy George, Pete Burns, and Cherry Bombs—set to puree.

Surprisingly, the Elders said nothing more. I suspect they loved Dad too much, and the fact that he tried everything they asked. I also believe that Michael Todd was a force greater than anything any of them had ever faced.

The show must go on! And it did—straight into the halls of the Christian Academy founded by our church. You know, the same church where Dad was the minister. Michael Todd was a student.

I can only imagine how many gray hairs the principal sprouted with Michael Todd's glittery little fingerprints all over them.

What do you do with a kid like that—especially when he's the preacher's son?! You pray for your sanity. That's what you do.

## The Great Tunic Incident

One day, Michael Todd showed up to school in full Boy George regalia—tunic, make-up, and all the trimmings. The principal called him to the office for wearing a "dress."

Michael's defense?

"It's a tunic, for Christ's sake. Even *HE* wore one! And I'm wearing leggings."

Despite his theologically sound fashion defense, they sent him home.

Sometime later, the administration expelled him for being too fabulous and a glittery trail of other infractions. The Christian school had become too limiting to handle his kind of circus.

What's now called Fabulous was then called a Freak Show, and not in the beautiful sense of that term.

So, he took the Freak Show to a new venue.

## Next Stop—The Public-School Edition

When the Midnight Circus rolled in, the bullies, who at this school were dressed as "jocks," didn't know what hit them. They were no match for his wicked-fast wit and his cunning use of the AIDS panic. Although he didn't have it, they didn't know. When threatened, he'd smirk:

"If you hit me, make sure I bleed... Who's up first?"

Not once was he touched.

Michael Todd attracted a band of glorious misfit toys who basked in his kaleidoscopic sphere of protection.

Meanwhile, I armed myself with football, girls, good grades, church chorus, and solos—all in the name of survival.

## "Why can't you be more like Jimmy?"

Being "more like Jimmy" was a game Michael Todd couldn't win—not that he needed or wanted to. But it had to sting.

I also used that line a time or two. I knew his life would be easier if he could be more like me. Not my proudest moment.

OK, already... enough about him. What about me?

# Girls, Girls, Girls… Meh

## What's All the Hoopla?

My older brother, John David, couldn't stop talking about girls, and that's all I heard my guy friends at school and church talking about. For some unknown reason, I had nothing to say, nothing to add to that conversation. I never had any crushes on girls.

One day after school, when we were around eleven years old, a girl named Angela had a bunch of us kids hanging out in her fort in the upper part of her garage. They started playing a game of strip-something, where articles of clothing would come off as you lost. They played, and I watched. For the first time, I saw a girl naked.

When I finally found out what all the hoopla was about underneath their clothes, it was like…Meh.

Even when my friends got hold of *Playboy* and other "dirty" magazines, nothing. No tingle. Not even a flicker. Not one inkling of interest. Ever.

## The Virginity Clause

Being a good boy and staying a virgin for my religion gave me the perfect excuse to avoid any trips south of the border with the young ladies. My "righteous belt of chastity" also kept the guys from teasing me about not scoring. It was a win-win. I got to keep my secret, and the girls got to keep their reputations and their "precious flowers" intact.

Word on the street? The girls were safe with me!

Growing up, I mostly hung out with girls, which confused people nicely. They assumed they were "girlfriends"—I didn't correct them.

## My "Tendencies" Trial

In college, my true self was ready to bust down the closet door—but my religion kept bolting it shut. One day, I cracked it open just enough to test my "tendencies" card on a sweet, naive, unsuspecting girlfriend.

"It's just a case of the tendencies," I told her, half hoping she'd help me step out of the closet for good. She helped me, alright—by trying to turn me into a "Ladies' Man!"

It didn't work. After several months of awkward failures, I accepted what my entire being already knew—I was, as I might put it, a "Man's Man."

*I will never put another woman through this again.*

That was my last attempt at trying to be something I wasn't.

## Looks Like We'll Need a Bigger Closet

Accepting that I was gay felt like a ten-ton, rainbow-colored elephant stepped off my chest. I named her Nellie. I could finally breathe. And then, what did I do? I climbed on top of Nellie's back and shoved that poor beast right back into the closet with me.

Even though I accepted it, I wasn't ready for the world to know.

"Come on, Nellie—suck in your gut. Looks like we'll need a bigger closet."

# The Big Gay Reveal

### No Shit!

After accepting the fact that I was a "Man's Man" during my senior year of college, I "came out" to Michael Todd. It was the first time I said the word "gay" outloud in reference to myself.

His reaction?

"No shit."

### Danger, Jimmy Belasco! Danger!

We compared childhoods. Yeah, not the best idea—and definitely don't compare a *Brady Bunch* childhood to someone who grew up in *The Land of the Lost. Oops.* That's precisely what I did—a direct comparison at that.

*Did we grow up with the same parents?*

He called me "completely delusional."

I mumbled, "Drama queen."

At the time, I was unaware of all that Michael Todd went through with the conversion attempts. It would have been a different conversation had I known. And yes, I do believe that's true. I wasn't a complete jerk—at least not yet.

Now that I know his past more fully, my life was definitely very much like The Brady Bunch compared to his *Land of the Lost*, but not a good point to make at the time.

## It's Getting Messy—I Mean, Late! I'm Out of Here!

He ended our conversation—and the entire evening—when he delivered the fatal blow. Something that would echo in my mind for decades:

"You're the most self-absorbed human I know."

"Alrighty... I'm out of here!" I said, ducking out before the unsolicited mirror he held up could expose any more.

It hurt because it was true.

At the time, I didn't see it that way. I just thought he was jealous and melodramatic, creating self-inflicted drama because his life was too dull.

Oh, jeez, was I wrong.

## The Golden Anvil

That night, he became the only person in my family who knew my secret.

A secret he held in his back pocket, right alongside his pain from all the privilege I held for living my lie.

What I didn't realize was that with that secret, I'd also handed him a weapon:

A Golden Anvil with my name engraved on it, in a glass box labeled:

"Break Glass in Case of Emergency!"

# Plotting My Demise

## You Do That Voodoo

I suspect Michael Todd began plotting my demise long before I brushed off his insights during our "big reveal," and my indifference to what I saw back then as his melodramatic life did nothing to help my case. So, I have this theory—scratch that, a full-on visual—of how his plotting might have looked. Picture it:

A white-washed basement with sweaty walls that look like they're weeping. There, in the flickering glow of candlelight, is Michael Todd wearing a heavily beaded, tattered wedding gown—a stitch-for-stitch replica of one he made for Miss Piggy—though his is soaked in tears, mascara mixed with glitter, and smells of revenge and Drakkar Noir.

In the middle of the room is an altar laden with clippings of my now strawberry-blonde hair, clandestine photos of me doing something overtly gay, and the partially burned remnants of that pink, poofy-sleeved pirate blouse I "lost" after my Coming Out Party.

In the corner, on top of a pedestal, sits that glass box holding the prized Golden Anvil—"In Case of an Emergency." One perfectly placed spotlight makes it glow.

Like a Voodoo priestess, he twirls dramatically around the altar as his voice crescendos into Boy George's finest, "Do You Really Want to Hurt Me?" And in the twisted b-roll of his mind, he's haunted by a sinister chant taunting him in my voice:

"Why can't you be more like Jimmy? ...more like Jimmy... like Jimmy..."

[Fade to black.] And Scene.

Was it real? Probably not.

Could it have been? Absolutely.

# Double, Double Toil and Trouble

### This Place is About to Blow!

After college, I moved back to Michigan and in with Michael Todd—and a witch who lived in the basement. Yes, I said a witch. Not just any witch. A self-proclaimed White Witch. Back then, I didn't know the difference between a white witch and any other kind of witch.

And when I say white, I mean WHITE. She wore white. She painted her face white. She even painted the entire basement white—walls, floors, ceilings, the whole thing—like she was living inside a snow globe. Her hair leaned yellow, but I think it, too, was an attempt at white.

"Live and let live" was my Dad's motto, and I agreed with it in theory. But this live-and-let-live situation was living in the basement. I admit, it was unsettling... probably for both of us. She had to deal with me—an uptight, semi-closeted, "pretty" boy wearing too much cologne, and stomping around upstairs in what would be the attic—my bedroom.

To be clear, she was nice as could be. Polite. Soft-spoken. But stepping into that basement lifted the hairs on the back of my neck. Did I mention it was entirely white?

For the sake of anonymity, let's call her Glinda, the Good White Witch, since I later learned white witches are known for good magic.

At the time, though, if the house felt like it might explode at any minute, I figured it had to be Glinda brewing something up.

But what was really brewing wasn't in the basement; it was upstairs in the attic, where I stayed.

## My Big Gay Life

Much of my life at that point was out of the closet, with one major exception: my family and the church we grew up in, where Dad still preached.

But my Big Gay Life was growing nightly.

Michael Todd was the reigning Queen of the Detroit Club Kids—an androgynous ringleader with a loyal crew of side-show freaks and circus clowns in tow. And now, I had the honor of being one of them. This time for me was freedom and fun personified.

I leaned into the role as his clean-cut older brother and unlikely sidekick. It worked. I loved every second of the ride.

Michael Todd & Jimmy, 1987.

Night after night, at clubs across the city, we weren't the Golden Child and the Black Sheep—we were the Fabulous Belasco Brothers, dancing the night away at the center of a fantastical universe swirling around us.

Look familiar? The cute guy on the right (and p. 52) is me.
Michael Todd dressed me up for a night of clubbing in Chicago, 1987.

FUN FACT: the root of a budding problem—we were both into the same type of guys—clean-cut, all-American. Michael Todd's industrialized fabulousness may have turned heads at the club, just not the ones he wanted. They looked at me instead. For once, being cute worked in my favor. But it worked against us.

At home, the energy shifted. I blamed Glinda and her spells.

Wrong again.

Years of my unspoken privilege, indifference, and one very heavy Golden Anvil had started burning a hole in Michael Todd's back pocket.

I didn't see it then—but something—or someone—in that house was ready to blow.

The something? A Golden Anvil.

The someone? Michael Todd.

The final straw? A clean-cut, all-American guy.

The target? Yours truly.

That house was bubbling with double, double, toil and trouble. And yes, the cauldron was my brother, and I was the one stirring the pot.

# The Final Straw

### Ready? ACTION!

On that fateful night, I was upstairs in my room, talking to a cute, clean-cut, all-American guy that Michael Todd also liked. This poor guy didn't know he'd landed a walk-on role in our long-running sibling rivalry scene—cast as "the final straw," given no lines, one dramatic close-up, and to be "written out" in just one scene.

Mid-conversation between me and Mr. All-American, Michael Todd, dramatically yelled up the stairs,

"Jim! Get down here now! I smashed my fingers in the trunk! You need to take me to the hospital! NOW!"

I figured it was just a ploy to ruin my evening with this cute guy. So, like the empathetic saint I am, I shouted back,

"Bull shit! Call someone who cares—I'm busy!"

Turns out, Michael Todd *had* smashed his fingers. Oops. But neither his fingers nor cutie-pie were the real issue.

When I finally peeked downstairs—a sight I'll never forget—there stood Michael Todd, his allegedly mangled fingers mysteriously out of sight. With one deliberate tap of his apparently good forefinger to his forehead—like pressing an "INITIATE" button—his demeanor flipped from melodramatic to terrifyingly composed. His voice, now cold, eerily calm, and an octave lower, similar to Hannibal Lecter's, sent a chill down my spine as he announced,

"Jim, I'm calling Mom now."

Mysteriously, a phone appeared in his hand as if summoned by spooky magic (or possibly a white witch just off-camera).

*Oh, shit!*

## Operation: Golden Boy!

Knowing with every fiber of my being that I should keep my mouth shut, I instead did the exact opposite.

"Go ahead, call Mom!" Fully aware, I made a fatal mistake.

It was like witnessing a sleeper agent activate. His eyes gleamed with calculated glee, and I swear I could hear his internal monologue:

"OPERATION GOLDEN BOY—INITIATE! Black Sheep is prepared to strike! The Golden Boy is going down! Repeat, THE GOLDEN BOY IS GOING DOWN!"

He started dialing.

I stopped breathing.

I remember the first 13 seconds of that call. Then everything went dark.

"Hi, Mom! Do you remember how everyone always wanted *me* to be more like *Jimmy*? Well, as it turns out, *Jimmy* is more like *me...*"

[Fade to black.]

I woke up sometime later in the prone position at the top of the stairs, in a pool of sweat and drool. The all-American cutie? Gone and never seen again. For the record, I thought Michael Todd and Glinda conjured a spell and made him disappear.

## Operation: Golden Boy—Target Neutralized

And that, my friends, is how you out your delusional, self-absorbed, moderately insufferable brother to your parents.

It wasn't a tantrum. It was a surgical strike—calculated, deliberate, and terrifyingly effective.

Michael Todd had waited years for the perfect opening.

His precision—chilling. His patience—quite impressive.

Anyone willing to "lie in wait" that long earns a twisted kind of respect.

I had no idea he had that in him. Now I do.

And I sincerely hope I never see that side of him again—unless he aims it at someone else who's not standing next to me.

Oddly enough, after that night, Michael Todd became my hero.

Our relationship shifted nearly overnight. I'm not sure how and why, but we became best friends.

Perhaps it opened my eyes to his side of the story. Maybe he just scared the living hell out of me, and this was survival instinct kicking in.

For him, maybe it was the release he needed.

Whatever it was, it worked.

I was 22. And this was the start of something new.

## RIP Pink Closet

Before I move on, I want to give a special shoutout to my well-fortified pink closet. It kept my secrets safe for over a decade, enduring years of near-discoveries, close calls, and overcrowding. And then, in one well-executed tactical move, Michael Todd blew it into pink goo-bits.

Rest in peace, my faithful companion. You served me well.

Luckily, Nellie was already out of the closet at the time of the implosion. She's alive and well to this day.

## My Parents' Reaction

After Michael Todd's decade-long Three-Ring Circus—thrills, spills, and enough scary clowns to keep our parents up at night—my coming out felt like the Tuesday Night Blue Plate Special at the local diner: overcooked, entirely unremarkable, and forgotten by the time I hit the door.

*Damn it. Outshined again!*

That said, surprisingly, it caught my entire family off guard. They were utterly clueless, which honestly felt like a badge of honor for my Wilderness Survival Skills in Acting. Managing that closet was rough—another merit pin for my Scout sash.

Aren't moms supposed to know these things before we do? Not mine.

Years of Oscar-worthy performances, and the payoff? A collective shrug.

"Are you sure, dear? Really? Okay. We're proud of you. Honey, you're blocking the TV. And could you change the channel on your way out? Channel 2. *Murder, She Wrote* is starting."

No fireworks. Just me, slipping offstage to polite applause.

All that dread, all that buildup—and *Murder, She Wrote* got top billing?

That's a lot of wasted closet time for just obligatory applause!

Come to think of it, there was a tear in Mom's eye, but I'm afraid she was probably just relieved I didn't arrive with fresh hoops for them to jump through. Michael Todd had already run them through enough flaming hoops for a lifetime.

### A Hero Dressed in Sheep's Clothing

Michael Todd's the hero here. He blazed the trail—smashed every wall—so I could stroll through the rubble, dust-free.

Because of the work he and my parents did, I stepped into this new part of my life surrounded by love, not interrogation and torment.

No condemnation. No clownselors lurking in the bushes.

I'm so grateful.

### The Timing was Right

Michael Todd gave our whole family a gift by outing me.

Before, I kept them at arm's length to control the narrative.

But now? Since I'm an avid oversharer, they got the whole messy, fabulous story.

And to my surprise, I loved telling it as much as they loved hearing it.

My openness then opened the door for Michael Todd to let the family in on his life as well. Yes, Michael finally forgave our parents for their sins.

Family gatherings around the fire pit became Big Gay Storytime— Michael Todd and I reliving our misadventures, while everyone laughed their asses off.

His infamous "Initiate" and "Strike" buttons didn't trigger the fireworks he initially intended...

But they set off a spectacular show that blew the lid off our family's silence—and lit up everything we'd been too afraid to show. We are free to be ourselves.

Gosh! I love my family!

So, thank you, Michael Todd, for being just vengeful enough that night and so loving ever since.

Operation: Golden Boy? Mission Complete. Success.

The fallout? Surprisingly fabulous.

Jimmy & Michael Todd.

# My Life Made Easier?

## Rough Roads Ahead

Picture it: Detroit, 1987. Mom's pearls? They would have helped, but I was still ducking them like they were dodgeballs. Instead, what I thought was wisdom was really just me confusing ego for arrival.

Thanks to Michael Todd, I was finally OUT.

Free to be me.

The problem? I had no idea who "me" was. And had no clue that I didn't know who I was.

I was heading into ROUGH ROADS AHEAD.

Sure, Michael Todd had made my life easier by bulldozing the path, but now I had no idea how to navigate these new waters.

While I polished my Golden Child façade, he was out there earning scars and building wisdom. Now it was my turn to do it the hard way. Well, my "hard way" was nothing compared with his; who am I kidding?

But I was still decades behind.

Of course, back then, I didn't see it that way.

I still thought I had it all figured out.

It's laughable now.

The closet may have exploded, but my delusional ego was fully intact and newly accessorized.

I was out, technically.

But was I free?

## Role Reversals—Twists and Turns

Michael Todd and I became best friends in the late 80s, shortly after he revealed my secret to my parents. It marked the beginning of a new era—and a new geography.

He moved to New York City. I headed to Dallas.

Our big leaps came with twists, turns, and a few moments of public vomiting. Yeah, that last one was me.

Toward the end of his Detroit club days, Michael Todd was a full-blown wild child. Most of the family didn't think he'd make it to 21. Honestly, neither did I.

When I visited him in New York, within his first year, he was struggling but working hard to make it there.

The club scene no longer held his attention. But I can't say the same. Now I was becoming the wild child.

He was growing up.

I was growing down.

We didn't talk much; I was too busy pretending to thrive in my new world. My dream life in Dallas was unraveling.

My custom clothing business was sustaining me, but I was making increasingly bad choices—party drugs and glow-sticks included.

Now I was the one teetering on the edge of self-destruction.

The Golden Child had officially entered his Fool's Gold era.

# Ring, Ring... Destiny Calling

## Was I Ready?

It's now around 1993, and it had been at least a year since I'd spoken with Michael Todd when we finally caught up on the phone. Something about him was different. His words carried a tone I hadn't heard before: calm, confident, oddly mystical. He kept talking about "calling forth," "manifesting," and "spirit guides." To me, it all sounded like hooey-dooey nonsense.

I hung up thinking, *Alrighty then—great for you, just don't get any of that nonsense on me.*

Six months later, we spoke again, and this time his mystical mumbo jumbo came with receipts. He walked into a New York City hair salon and left as their Master Colorist—complete with the previous colorist's clientele and a six-figure income.

Meanwhile, I was manifesting unpaid invoices and self-loathing. I was a bit jealous. Actually, I was a lot jealous.

Was this the same Michael Todd who'd several times turned my hair beige-green, red, blue, blue-green, and orange back in beauty school just a few years earlier? Now he was "manifesting" six figures for hair color? My Golden Child ego hated it. And this miraculous dream job was just a highlight of the many magical things happening in his life. I was about to hang up when he said:

"Do you want to meet me in Los Angeles? One of my spirit guides told me there's a *key* waiting for me there. I think you're supposed to join me. Come on, it'll be fun."

Hocus pocus or not, a trip to LA sounded like the distraction I needed. "Sure, let's go find your magical little key."

### Lucille Ball's Haunted House

The first and main thing on Michael Todd's LA to-do list? Lucille Ball's Roxbury Drive mansion. It was several years after her death, and the family had just sold the estate. He'd heard that the house was slated for demolition, and being forever Lucy-obsessed, he had to see it before it vanished. He had Lucy tattooed on his arm and had won many Halloween contests dressed as her. Lucy was a significant influence on both of us. I carried on the Halloween tradition, winning costume contests in Dallas over several years.

Lucy (Michael), John (my ex), & Ethel (me). Wigstock—NYC, 1994.

My twist on a Beatles' song & Lucy. Halloween, 1996.

Michael Todd's Lucy untucked, 1994.

When we pulled up, Michael Todd drifted out of the car like he was in a trance. A woman in a housekeeper's uniform sat at the top of the driveway, by the gate. Next thing I knew, he was up there talking to her, and she waved him inside the gate into Lucy's compound.

*What the—?* I grabbed my disposable camera, scrambled out of the car, and hoofed it up the driveway. As I approached the woman, she said, "Lucy's house," as she motioned me in like we were expected guests. Janet, our friend and driver, chose to stay in her car.

By the time I crossed under the drive-through archway, Michael Todd was already at the back door, about to step inside the house.

"Michael! What are you doing?"

"She said I could go in," he shrugged.

"Caaaarrrs!" I dramatically pointed at the row of expensive cars parked inside the compound.

"They're moving out, Jim. They're between trips, nobody's home. Come on, let's check it out!"

And just like that, we were inside Lucille Ball's house. Fully unattended.

## A Madcap Adventure—Lucy Style

I was geeking out and freaking out—even though the woman in uniform invited us in, it felt like we were going to get caught. Michael Todd, meanwhile, was in a state of Zenful bliss. We were exploring the house of one of the world's most famous people—by ourselves! I was standing in the room where an *I Love Lucy* episode was filmed, with her hiding under a bear rug, supposedly in a famous Hollywood star's home—Richard Widmark.

The front door opened. We froze. Footsteps. My lungs quit.

*We're caught—it's over!*

"Oh, thank goodness, Janet, it's you!" Janet walked in and said, "What are you doing down here? Let's find her bedroom. I'll bet it's upstairs."

We all ran upstairs, somehow knowing where to go—straight to it.

Next thing I knew, we were on the balcony outside Lucy's bedroom, overlooking her backyard, or compound. I was looking down at the patio, the very spot where I once saw an interview.

Then, we found her bathroom!

Lucy's bathroom was pure Lucy—all white and mirrors with pink sinks, toilet, bidet, and a large pink sunken bathtub. Michael Todd climbed into the tub for a picture... snap! Then on the toilet—why? I don't know, but... snap! Meanwhile, I was seeing spots—not from the photos. I stepped out into the bedroom to catch my breath; my head was spinning from the cocktail of fear and joy I was downing. (I can't find those photos.)

That's when I heard it—coming from the bathroom.

CLINK... CLANK.

I popped back in.

Michael was unscrewing a drawer knob from the vanity.

"MICHAEL?!" I was down to monosyllables at this point.

"They're tearing this place down in two weeks. You think I'm leaving empty-handed?"

"JAIL!" Two octaves higher than normal.

"Do you want one?" he grinned.

(One Mississippi, Two Mississippi...) "...YES!?"

By Three Mississippi, I was a full accomplice. Now I was hunched over, unscrewing as if my life depended on it, and rambling—full sentences.

"I'm going to prison. I'll be BITCH BAIT! I'll never make it in there!" All the while, I pictured myself as the "wife" of some guy named Big Billy, trading cigarettes and "favors" for survival.

Michael, as if it were just a normal Tuesday afternoon, tucked the knobs into his underwear, giving himself a massive, yet awkward-looking porn-star-sized bulge.

"You don't think they'll notice that?!" I hissed.

We hit the grand staircase and slipped out the side door. Janet's intuition had the getaway car waiting up at the top of the driveway by that side door, right where the uniformed woman sat. I dove in through the open window into the back seat like I was Bonnie and he was Clyde. Although it was probably more like I was Ethel and he was Lucy. Michael strolled, waved at the housekeeper, and slid into the front seat like he was leaving a dinner party. "Thank you!"

"Slowly back down the driveway," he instructed Janet, calm as ever.

## The Longest Driveway

My heart pounded like a timpani drum in the middle of a crescendo. That driveway seemed to stretch for miles. Just as we neared the street, a car pulled forward, blocking the exit.

*I knew it. This is it! I don't want to be Big Billy's wife!*

We sat frozen. Trapped.

"Should we peel across the lawn?" I said, panicked.

"No, shhhh. Relax." Michael Todd insisted.

Then the housekeeper started walking down the driveway toward us.

*Holy shitballs! It's a sting operation!*

She waved as she passed our car and slipped into the waiting car.

*Her ride! Not the cops!*

"Hallelujah!" I exhaled.

Janet eased us onto the street, smooth as silk. I didn't breathe again until we were out of Beverly Hills.

Before you judge our little madcap caper, hear me out. Rumor had it Lucy's ghost still lingered there. To this day, we fully believe that Lucy's ghost orchestrated the whole thing.

Those two little vanity knobs? Gifts. From Lucy herself. And with the house headed for demolition, there's a good chance they would have been part of the rubble.

I know this sounds like something right out of an *I Love Lucy* script, but that's how it happened.

I couldn't wrap my brain around it. Luckily, my brother and Janet were there, so I didn't think it was a dream.

## The Real Key

Once we were safely out of the neighborhood, we screamed as if we'd just won the lottery. The energy inside the car made it feel as if the wheels weren't touching the ground.

Once we calmed down, we all remained silent for a while, reliving the experience. The silence was broken when Michael Todd turned around, held up one of the knobs, and grinned. We simultaneously said:

"The key."

He handed it to me, "I believe this one is yours."

Never mind that it had just been in his sweaty banana hammock—I held it like it was the Hope Diamond. It wasn't just a knob; it felt like a key to my future. The key to what? Not a clue.

I went home to Dallas with that "key" in my pocket and a mind blown wide open.

*How did we show up at the precise moment when they were between trips, leaving the house empty? Why had the family housekeeper let us inside, alone? Was Lucy's ghost our host? What magical force had Michael Todd tapped into?*

I had too many questions, so I set aside my Golden Child ego and called him.

"OK, Michael Todd. What's going on, what's your secret?"

## Stuart Smalley, Are You Kidding?

"Do you remember that book I gave you for Christmas a couple of years ago?" he said.

Oh, *that* book? I couldn't dare tell him, but it went straight to the trash bin the moment I read the back cover.

"Sure, yeah, I still have that book. But Michael, it's about *affirmations*? That's all just a joke, right?"

Affirmations had become a joke on SNL with a character named Stuart Smalley. His signature mock-earnest affirmation:

*"I'm good enough, I'm smart enough, and doggone it, people like me."*

Yeah, no. Hard pass.

Michael Todd just laughed. "Call them mantras if it helps. Trust me, Jim. They work."

"I don't know, Michael..." Then I thought, *I just took a magical carpet ride through Lucy's house with more questions than I have answers for... Shut up, Jimmy!* "Okay, fine. What's the name of the book again? Ah... ah, so I can find it... in my library?" Liar, liar—I didn't have a library.

"The book is *You Can Heal Your Life* by Louise Hay. And by the way, Jim, you can buy another copy at any bookstore."

*Damn it, how does he know when I'm lying?*

## A Mantra, A New Beginning

I bought the book. I read the book. It changed the course of my life nearly immediately. Within that first week, my best friend and I came up with a business idea, and everything fell into place like magic.

My first self-affirming "mantra" was simple:

*"I am open and receptive to all the Love, Abundance, Success, Serenity, and Opportunities the Universe has to offer."* L.A.S.S.O.

LASSO—had all my bases covered—Love, Abundance, Success, Serenity, and Opportunities.

That first business turned out to be my first candle company. Our rise was meteoric.

The Golden Child was back on top—but this time, with a bit of help from a little black sheep and a ghost named Lucy.

# My Candle Era Begins

## We Backed into It

It was the early 90s, when my hair was almost as high as my ego. I thought I was living the dream—new company, plenty of friends, endless parties with plenty of party favors. I even had my mantras. But that's about as deep as it got.

Our "big" idea was to take unknown artists' products to national wholesale markets, make sales for the artists, and earn commissions—we all get rich. We had dozens of products, everything from rolled beeswax candles to hammocks, like a world market exploded in our booth. The only things we actually made ourselves were these tiny glass votives, each covered in composite gold leaf with a moody patina, for use with candles. We called the line Alchemy. Pretty, yes, but we assumed the rolled beeswax candles from one of our artists would be the star.

That's not what happened.

At our first round of trade shows, those little Alchemy votives took center stage. Several national shows and broken samples later, we had exactly one sample left for our last show in San Francisco. On the second-to-last day, the Nordstrom fragrance buyer walked in, beelined for our lone survivor, and ordered 4,500 boxed sets of two. That's 9,000 votives. The caveat we agreed to was that each would need to include a hand-poured scented candle.

After the buyer left our booth, we grabbed each other and jumped up and down, trying to muffle our screams. This elation lasted only about 30 seconds before we started thinking about the labor-intensive process involved in creating that finish—9,000 times! On top of that, we didn't know how to pour candles—we'd have to get someone else to pour them for us. We weren't sure whether to laugh or cry, but we got our first major retailer order.

We found a pourer three hours away from where we lived, but my partner's SUV could hold only 1,000 votives. We had 9,000. That's nine round-trips, if you're into third-grade math. Meanwhile, every votive needed handwork—gluing, wrapping, and oxidizing brass "gold" leaf—in our Texas carport. Carpal tunnel and heat stroke, anyone? Gold flecks drifted throughout the neighborhood. We delivered on time. By the next show, six months later, our Alchemy votives expanded into a full collection. Sales skyrocketed. We bought a book, taught ourselves to pour candles, ditched the "representing artists" idea, and—whoops— became a candle company.

## Mad Scientist

If you'd seen me back then, "mad scientist" would've been dead-on. I wasn't a scientist, but I was crazed for sure—fueled by caffeine, American Spirit cigarettes, and the need to fix every candle flaw on earth: tunneling, weak scent, sooty flames.

Then I heard about Michael Richards, who'd invented a 100% vegetable wax from soybeans—patent still pending at the time. Soy wax. Renewable, clean-burning, and not relying on fossil fuels like paraffin wax. Months later, Michael Richards, the inventor of soy wax, walked into my New York booth. *Jimmy, pay attention.* I became one of his first and most enthusiastic customers.

Soy was stubborn, but so was I. My worktable became a wax-splattered crime scene, and I drove my perfumer insane.

But I knew—soy wax was the future of the candle industry.

## The Candle Industry

For over a century, paraffin ruled the candle world, made from crude oil. "Big Oil" execs even sat on the National Candle Association (NCA) board. When I started marketing soy and highlighting paraffin's downsides, the NCA sent me a cease-and-desist letter. I replied with a stack of hard facts. They went silent.

By the mid-90s, "renewable" was becoming a buzzword, and Big Oil wasn't happy with me. I knew I was onto something.

## Setbacks, Mantras, and the Right Call

Just as I geared up to launch my soy line, our company collapsed—there was no fixing it. We had to close our doors. I could barely get out of bed. But somewhere in the rubble, a voice rose within me:

*I will turn this into the best thing that could have happened for me.*

I started a new company in six weeks. Just one week before we were to launch the line at the first of the national markets, a major investor—over half of my capital—bailed. Determined, I called it forth:

*"I'm calling forth an investor who has the financial strength and knowledge to guide the company financially so that I can introduce soy to the world. Oh, and I need them to appear, like tomorrow—market starts next week."*

I was half kidding about the "tomorrow" part and 100% serious about the rest. It actually happened.

The next day, someone I hadn't spoken to in years called, wanting to go into the candle business with me. The strangest part was that both business partners woke up with the same idea. What they came to the table with was exactly what I had called forth—less than 24 hours earlier.

They said, "We can provide the funding and guide the company financially," using nearly the same words as I had called forth, "and you can drive the company creatively." They were unaware that I called this forth and was ready to go to market the following week.

Coincidence? Never. We struck a deal, and I was back on track. We arrived at the markets on schedule.

*Perhaps this manifesting stuff really does work!*

That was all the proof I needed. I became a confident and masterful manifestor for the next decade.

## Pioneering Soy Candles

From the mid-90s to early 2000s, my climb felt glacially slow. Industry friends whispered that soy was a waste of time—"...it's just a fad." I was the only one of my candle peers who believed soy wax was the future of candles. I spent my time educating the public and retailers in the gift and spa industry. My soy candles and stories about what I was doing were eventually in hundreds of magazines. These were the days before the internet could make things go viral overnight—print publications were the primary best route.

Then came 9/11/2001—infamously known as 9/11. It was as if there was a shift in consciousness. Almost overnight, people began to care more about what they brought into their homes and into their bodies. Companies selling healthier products, such as Whole Foods, took off—and so did my candles. My years of educating the retailers and the public worked. The stars aligned. I was ready. It paid off—big time.

The Soy Candle Revolution had finally begun, and I was out there in front. The new question at every register: "Are these soy candles?"

I didn't invent soy wax, but I helped drag it into the mainstream. I was even featured on CNN's TV program, NewsNight, a few years later. I felt like the King of Soy Candles. Nobody else was, so I took the title.

The soy candle category is now a multi-billion-dollar industry, with cumulative global sales. Not bad for a "fad." You're welcome, world.

That sounds a bit cocky, but once you hear the rest of the story, you'll understand that it isn't. And, to be clear, only a small fraction of those billions landed in my bank.

But still, you're welcome.

# A Dingo Ate My Baby, I Went on a Cruise

By 2005, my majority shareholders and I were going in different directions. They owned the majority. I owned the vision. We were no longer a match. Walking away from my baby gutted me. But once again, I reframed:

*I am turning this into the best thing that could have happened for me.*

Not knowing what my next business move should be, I went on a cruise. My ritual: step away, clear my head, call it forth, and let the answers come to me. On day one of the cruise, I declared:

*"I'm calling forth the IDEA, the PLAN, and the INNOVATION for what's next."*

And then I let it go. My mind was on the present moment—that cruise. Not what happened. Not what I wanted to happen. Instead, it was buffets, naps, portside villages, and cheesy shows that filled my days and nights. By the final night—like magic—it landed.

The *idea*. The *plan*. The *innovation*.

It all came to me in what felt like a fully formed information bubble.

By now, I had become a walking, Magical Manifesting Machine. In fact, that is what I started calling my ability to manifest.

## Five and a Half Weeks

I got off that ship with nothing but a fully formed vision. Five and a half weeks later, it was all real: a new company, a new brand, seventeen new fragrances, six national showrooms, fifty-some-odd reps, and packaging that would go on to win Best New Product for Packaging Innovation at the New York International Gift Fair. It felt like accepting an Oscar.

My booth at the NY International Gift Fair

My Magical Manifesting Machine had done it again.

Oh yeah—let me explain briefly what that is.

## My Magical Manifesting Machine

Magical Manifesting Machine is what I call the built-in system that we all have.  You've got one. I've got one. Scientifically sound.

It's built into our "wiring" and runs constantly, quietly shaping our lives whether we realize it or not. The process starts with *our thoughts* and is fueled by *our emotions* and *beliefs*. The "magical" part kicks in when we begin operating it intentionally. Life starts reflecting your choices instead of your chaos.

This book isn't the place for all the details, but after this next chapter, you'll see what can happen when fear starts to fuel the machine.

# John and the Jerk

### Guess Who's the Jerk?

John and I met in our twenties, back in 1994, right as I was starting my first candle company. He was gorgeous, with a face that resembled Leonardo DiCaprio's, and hair like Michelle Pfeiffer's. I looked more like Drew Carey's stunt double. Still, together we looked like quite the pair—long-standing fixtures in our social circles, bonded by a twisted sense of humor.

He had to have a sense of humor to survive my selfish years. Because let's face it: I was a jerk.

## My Selfish Years

Our fifteen-year relationship ran simultaneously with the rise and fall of my candle career, and I can say without hesitation—I had no grasp of selflessness, at least at first. I exposed my selfishness on our second date, the infamous "pizza story." John got a lot of mileage out of that one.

It was the spring of 1994. I'd ordered a pizza and asked John to pick it up on his way over to my place. It was pouring rain—that's why I asked. He arrived at my porch an hour late, drenched, holding the soggy box like a life preserver. I opened the door, grinned, and said:

"Thank goodness you're here, I'm starving! What took you so long?"

Without waiting for an answer, I snatched the pizza box, grabbed a slice, and walked away, eating it—leaving him standing on the front porch.

No "welcome," no "thank you," and no "let me get you a towel to dry off."

As if that wasn't enough, I hadn't prepaid for the pizza. The place only took cash, and evidently, I'd failed to mention that to John. When he arrived at the pizza place, they informed him of the amount due and the *cash-only* policy. He had no cash, so he had to head back out into the storm, hunting for an ATM. No umbrella. In and out of the car. Soaked all over again. Adding to my jerkdom, I never offered to reimburse him.

How could I have been such a horrible person?

I would have bolted from the pizza place when they handed me the bill. But John came back. And he stayed—fifteen years.

He loved retelling that story at parties—always to roars of laughter and my mock-shame. His punchline was always the same:

"You know why I stuck around? I wanted to make him fall in love with me so I could ruin his life."

I still chuckle thinking about it. As John tells it, he stood on the porch, watching me walk away, while he looked around for cameras to see if he was on the TV show *Punked*.

"What took you so long?" I was such an ass!

That moment was a solid SASS Level 4.0—off the charts!

I think that was a pivotal moment. I was so ridiculously self-centered, and John didn't let me get away with it. He made sure I saw who I was over the next fifteen years.

## Why He Stayed?

I'm not sure why John stayed. I must have shifted somewhere right about then, or he would have never stayed around. John doesn't put up with that level of idiocy.

Maybe at first it was just to torture me for a while? I guess he figured it would either ruin my life or change it.

But he didn't stick around for fifteen years to ruin my life and tell the pizza story. For a decade, we laughed every day, traveled the world, and filled our lives with friends and family. I loved his family, and he loved mine. He could be dramatic, sharp-tongued, and occasionally outrageous—but he was also steady, and fiercely protective of me.

One of his greatest attributes is his love of animals. That may have saved me as much as it saved the animals we rescued. Soon after that horrible second date, John and I rescued our first animal—a cat named George, who stayed at my place. A year later, when we moved in together, two rescue dogs joined the family within the first week. Then came the strays, the injured, and the ones left for dead. Somehow, they all found us; some literally just showed up at our house. One walked in the front door, looked around, and made himself comfortable. Our family grew to thirteen dogs and that cat named George. However, we probably found homes for another dozen or so dogs.

Those animals opened my heart to compassion and selflessness, slowly growing one new family member at a time. Perhaps it was this newfound compassion that softened my rough edges, making me a little more likable, maybe even lovable.

Maybe that's why John stayed for fifteen years—I was learning to love like a dog.

I know I slipped in and out of being that jerk. But I also know I left that relationship a better person—by light-years—than when we started. The compassion I learned from John, along with my love for our fur family, softened my heart. Perhaps he stayed because he could see a better version of me starting to emerge, even when I couldn't. Or maybe—just maybe—he stayed to show me what compassion looked like, and teach me some, because I needed it.

As you'll see throughout this story, John is still very much a part of my life. We had our rough patches, but now—over thirty years later—we're like two loving brothers who would do anything for each other. You may be surprised by how he's woven into my journey all the way through to the present. We'll get to that later.

# Losing Everything

## Double Implosion

Just because you think you've mastered the manifesting machine doesn't mean it always runs smoothly—it depends on what's fueling it.

I learned the hard way: fear and delusion make lousy fuel.

For years, my Magical Manifesting Machine drove me to the top of the candle world. I helped change the face of an industry. I was unstoppable.

And then the bottom dropped out—literally—the economic market.

Coming home from the January 2008 Gift Show in Atlanta, I faced the truth: the U.S. economy had flushed. Middle-class, gift-heavy stores vanished overnight. Customers disappeared. Sales cratered. My business was hemorrhaging, and the funding spigot had shut off.

And right alongside it, my fifteen-year relationship with John was unraveling in lockstep.

## The Relationship Implosion

Here's the thing: for a decade, John and I were mostly good. We laughed every day, traveled, rescued animals, and built a life together. But in the final five years, something shifted. The closeness evolved into a companionship. We still got along; we still made each other laugh—but we were living more separate lives.

John & Jimmy, 2002.

The more successful I became, the more physically unhealthy I became. My disdain for my body also didn't help our physical relationship. Looking in the mirror made me sick. *Who could love a body like this?* I shut down my physical affection.

Adding to that fixation, I had slipped back into another obsession, especially after I had to walk away from one business and launch a new one. It was game on, and I was all in—everyone else was out.

John filled his time with friends and trips. There were times he'd say, "If you cared half as much about me as you do your business..." And the truth is, I don't remember the rest of that sentence. I was probably wondering if my new candle needed more patchouli.

By the time my company began its freefall in 2008, our relationship was already paper-thin.

One day, while I was showering off the weight of the collapsing candle market, John strolled into the bathroom.

"We should start seeing other people," as casual as ordering takeout.

My knees buckled. "Do we have to do this right now?"

In a one-two gut punch, the two central pillars of my life that had coexisted simultaneously over the past fifteen years—my business and my relationship—cracked and crumbled at the same time.

## The Fear Revealed

I thought I was fearless. I'd lived that way for so long—charging ahead mindlessly—that my delusion wouldn't let me see it.

Not long after the market collapse and John's announcement, I was venting to a friend about my business. Their response?

"What are you so afraid of?"

Without missing a beat, equal parts cocky and clueless, I said,

"You know I don't operate from a place of... fear..."

But that last word caught in my throat.

It was as if someone had flicked on a light. For a split second, I saw the truth: I wasn't fearless at all. Brilliance didn't build the latest version of my empire. It was stacked brick by brick on fear—fear of losing everything I'd built. And that was well underway. I was deep in a well, built by those bricks of fear.

And just as quickly, the light flickered out.

Everything I allowed to define me—my successes, my business, my relationship, my image—was crumbling. And waiting at the bottom of that well was my new companion, darkness.

# Welcome to My Dark Period

### Hello Darkness, My New Friend

I'd never known depression growing up—at least not the kind that swallows you. Sure, I'd had my bouts of self-loathing in the mirror, and some major disappointments, but this was different. This was a free fall into something with no reference.

When I mentioned the deep, dark well, that wasn't an exaggeration. It was deep and dark, with no imaginable route of escape. The light above me shrank to a pinprick and then disappeared completely.

Days and nights blurred into each other. Getting out of bed wasn't just hard; it felt pointless. The world was muffled, as if I were moving under water, but inside my chest and head, everything was loud—panic, fear, and a crushing void all at once.

I didn't know what to call it at the time. Now I call it my Dark Period. Back then, it just felt like being buried alive.

### How Dark Can Dark Get?

To rub salt in my karmic wounds, neither my business nor my relationship ended cleanly—they died slow, painful deaths. The company limped along without funding for three more years while John and I were still stuck living under the same roof, trapped by the financial disaster we were enduring. I remember thinking,

*How dark can dark get?*

## Egg Sandwiches, Thirteen Dogs, and a Cat Named George

I clung to that dying company like I was trying to resuscitate a corpse. One by one, I let go of employees until only one was left: Maggie, John's mom—the one with the open-toed shoes.

Maggie, already my best friend, became a mother figure during those years. Amazingly, she helped me grieve both my relationship with her son and my company. She brought light when everything else felt hopeless: egg sandwiches, morning walks, and simply showing up with leftovers.

Not surprisingly, out of shame, my ego wouldn't let me turn to my mom.

And then there were our animals, the ones John and I rescued together: Sausage, Biscuit, Pepper, Sonny & Cher, Rusty Bumpers, Daisy Duke, Baxter, Hippity Hop, Chastity, Jelly Belly, Lucky, Baby—and George, the cat. Seeing all those wagging tails every day was like being wrapped in a warm hug and a reason to keep going.

My friend Joel, who lived with me for a while and helped make candles, also kept the house alive. All of their unconditional love fueled me, even when it felt like the world was pitch black inside my head.

## The Lowest Point

Facing that failing company every day was torture. My ego, welded to the business, was ground to dust. I felt worthless. I knew the company was dying, but I couldn't let go. Investors had trusted me, and the thought of failing them was unbearable. I was like a shipwreck survivor clinging to a sinking raft.

By the summer of 2009—about a year and a half in—my dying company weighed on me like an anchor. I was over 250 pounds, living on 99-cent double-cheeseburgers and cola.

It was so dark inside my head, I couldn't stand anything positive—even Oprah was too much light. That was not like me. I loved Oprah.

For the first time in my life, I experienced hopelessness.

Me—the face of depression.

### Losing My Machine

Here's the strangest part: I forgot I even had a Magical Manifesting Machine. Me—the guy who had built companies, manifested opportunities, and willed crazy dreams into reality—forgot my own machine existed. POOF! It was gone.

That's what depression did to me. It didn't just drain my hope—it wiped my memory clean of the very tools that could save me. I wasn't thinking about manifesting or mindset. I wasn't thinking at all. Half the time, I wasn't sure if I was wearing underwear.

What had blinded me was fear. Fear so heavy it fogged everything. Fear so loud, it drowned out everything I knew that could help me.

## The Pipe Dream

But even in the depths, a ridiculous idea floated up:

*What if a candle company licensed my brand?*

The idea was that they'd handle production, sales, and distribution—the parts crushing me—while I kept creative control and earned royalties. Most of all, it would require no additional funding from me for these efforts.

It was perfect. So perfect it felt laughable. Nobody in the candle industry had ever done this, to my knowledge. It was a total pipe dream, the kind of idea you laugh at and then bury before it breaks your heart. I buried it as quickly as I could.

Except it wouldn't stay buried. That little spark kept tapping me on the shoulder, refusing to die with the rest of my dreams.

## Finding My Machine Again

One night, sitting in the wreckage of my life, I thought:

*My fear-fueled thoughts brought me down to this point. What if I thought differently?*

It was as if the light had flicked back on. There it was, my machine, waiting for me. I didn't even need to dust it off; it looked shiny and new.

*I'd forgotten all about you!*

I knew the ropes; I'd done it hundreds of times. I took a deep breath, climbed back into the driver's seat, turned the key, and set a clear intention:

*"I'm calling forth a company to license my brand—they'll run production, sales, and distribution. I'll keep ownership, creative direction, and earn royalties."*

I sent it out into the universe—and I let it go. I told no one. Because, as I've learned, the magic happens when I set my intent and expect the result; I don't need to knock down doors.

## The Phone's for You—It's Your Pipe Dream

A month later, my phone rang. On the other end was the assistant to the owner of a larger candle company, one I was quite familiar with. They wanted to discuss—wait for it... what?

A licensing deal.

I had to sit down.

They had no idea what I'd been manifesting. They found me.

When we met, the terms matched exactly what I'd envisioned. We signed the contract, and they provided me with a budget to create a new collection. In just two months, we were at the national markets—on time, with my entire line and a fresh collection.

Freedom. For the first time in years, the weight that had been pulling me under started to lift. It wasn't the end of my darkness, but it was a light at the end of a very long, very dark tunnel.

# Letting Go

## Life is But a Stream

Over the years, I have come to understand the importance of letting go. Letting go allows me to move forward. An image I hold in my head is that life is a stream; it will take me where I need to go—if I let go. As I try to hold onto the branches, the things that no longer serve me, the water builds around me. If I don't let go, it will overwhelm me, and I will drown.

In 2010, with the licensing deal underway, I was free to think about something other than the hellhole in which I'd been living. But with that freedom came a surprising realization over the course of that year, and it helped explain some of the darkness I was still living with:

*There's no passion within me for my company—it's no longer me.*

Even though another company was running the daily operations, clinging to my brand felt like clinging to old energy, powered by a delusional ego I no longer obeyed. I didn't feel like the same person anymore, and to move forward, I knew I had to let the company go to achieve my ultimate freedom.

When the licensing contract was up for renewal at the end of that year, I dissolved it, closed my company, and finally drifted down the stream—not with dread, but with a sense of peace.

One of my friends asked, "Why so abruptly?"

"What you didn't see were the torturous years I spent trying to save a story that I now realize isn't mine anymore."

It was like Frank Sinatra and his hit song, "Strangers in the Night,"—which he hated—and having to sing it for the rest of his life, well past its expiration date.

For me, holding onto that company was soul-crushing.

## A Burst of Light

Walking away from my third and final candle company felt like a significant crumbling of the walls of my well of fear. It was as if I could finally focus on myself. I still had some darkness because I didn't quite know who I was anymore, I was "unemployed" and had a lot of dogs and the cat named George feed. But I no longer felt controlled by my past.

My ego, built on image and success, was destroyed along with all I built with it. It is a strange feeling when you stand at the core of who you are, without the ego that drove you to madness. It seemed like I was seeing the world through a completely different, sharper-focused lens.

It was both unnerving and exciting, yet simultaneously satisfying and terrifying. As I stepped away with nothing, and I mean nothing, I realized I had left behind a legacy.

My work in the candle industry has contributed to the planet's sustainability movement, helping educate a global audience and spark change. That realization brought a sense of closure and joy, allowing me to step into the nothingness as I began my next phase... whatever that might be.

Although I've mentioned my successes, I do so for reference and historical purposes. I no longer base my self-worth upon them. All of it is just a part of my past that helped me become someone I now love.

But I don't want to jump ahead too fast. Let's see how I got there.

# The Little Trick That Saved My Ass

## I'm Not a Scientist

Yes, it's true—I'm not a scientist. But the science behind why things work fascinates me.

During the final year of my business, when the licensing deal kicked in, I finally had free time and started exploring something beyond self-loathing. That something, as you might've guessed with that lead-in, was science.

It turns out that quantum physics and neuroscience, the two that I dug into the most, and a few other fields, explain the mechanics of the manifesting process I once thought was purely mystical. Please be patient while I geek out for a moment—this stuff excites me.

I discovered Dr. Candace Pert, a neuroscientist who blew my "pretty" little mind open. She demonstrated that *our thoughts* and the emotions around them produce chemical messengers in the body that help shape who we become, illustrating the connection between what we think and who we become.

Suddenly, thoughts weren't just ethereal—they were matter; they were chemistry. Our thoughts are powerful. They are the engine of our self-creation.

I didn't need scientific proof—I'd lived it. However, it was exciting to know that there is science behind it: My THOUGHTS create who I am and who I will become.

### A Preacher, a Scientist, and a "Pretty" Boy Walk into a Bar

All of this science talk sounded a lot like what Dad used to preach, and I experienced. It was all coming together.

- I call it my Magical Manifesting Machine.
- Dad calls it Proverbs 23:7, "As a man thinks in his heart, so is he."
- Dr. Pert calls it science: "What you *think* with *emotion* creates neuropeptides that flood your cells, and you become these thoughts."

Suddenly, the preacher, the scientist, and the "pretty" boy were all on the same page:

*What we think and believe in our hearts—we become.*

### The Little Trick

Which brings me to the trick. Let's wind back to the 1990s, shall we?

About a decade and a half before the science bomb hit me, I started experimenting with something from Louise Hay's book, *You Can Heal Your Life*, which Michael Todd had given me, and that I later had to repurchase.

Louise advised repeating affirmations with emotion and meaning until you start to believe them, which is supposed to happen naturally. When this happens, you start to become them.

Painfully simple. Possibly ridiculous. But I was desperate enough to try.

*If "I hate my body and my life" is running the show for me, what's the most profound thing I could repeat to reset my inner belief to the opposite? What could my life look like if I loved myself?*

I came up with "I love me" and started repeating it over and over.

At the time, I didn't love myself. Not even close. I wouldn't have been smoking, drinking, drugging, and overeating if I had. So I treated it like math. A numbers game. Say it enough times—believe it or not—and let's see what happens. I had nothing to lose.

With Michael Todd's endorsement and our magical carpet ride through Lucy's house in mind, I dove in. Loudly. Silently. Sometimes I found myself sobbing in traffic. Yes, ugly crying as I tried to drown out the negative sound bites in my head with something healthier.

I even made up a jingle.

> I love me, I love me, I'm wild about myself...
> I love me, I love me, I'm focused on my health...
> And when I'm feeling lousy, I stop and think, and say...
> I love me today!

You might have thought I was a little bit Cocoa Puffs. Maybe I was.

SNL could've made a skit about me. Move over, Stuart Smalley!

Shockingly, my body responded. However, I was oblivious to it for at least a week. One morning, sitting down with my business partner for coffee and my usual American Spirit cigarette—"all natural" cigarettes with no chemicals added, so at my funeral they could say I died of natural causes—I gagged and nearly threw up. That was not my usual response to my morning cigarette with coffee.

I figured the pack had gone bad, so I tried another, and another. Same result. Still not getting that what I'd been working toward with my "I love me" mantras was working, over the next week, the cigarettes, booze, drugs, and even food binges started making me sick. All those things that were harming me lost their appeal—my body was rejecting them. I soon stopped them all.

I started thinking about going for walks instead of doing bong hits while watching Food Network and raiding the cupboards for snacks. Believe it or not, I once considered having a salad for lunch. I tried it. It somehow satisfied me.

After a week of my mind and body responding differently, in healthier ways, I almost wrecked my car when it finally hit me:

*OMIGOSH! It worked...it's working!*

This ridiculous little trick, set to "I love me," rewired the toxic tape I'd been playing since I was a kid. I was so excited, I had to call Michael Todd.

His reply? "I told you so."

## The Seed

I'm not saying this was a one-and-done trick. Apparently, if you begin repeating the negative self-talk, guess what happens? Yeah, I did that.

Luckily, this experience with "I love me" and the results I achieved in the 90s planted the seed that pulled me out of the darkest chapter of my life 15 years later. Yep, we're jumping back to the future.

# Goodbye Darkness, My Old Friend

### Time for You to Move On

Fast-forward to late 2010, still in the midst of the licensing deal and just before closing my business, I was still lost in the shadows of darkness, but some light was beginning to peek in. That memory, seeded in the 90s, *the little trick*, popped in my head. It sparked something. If the mantra was effective back then, perhaps it could work again.

By that time, thanks to Dr. Pert, Louise Hay, and psychologists like Bandura and Helmstetter, who all agreed through different lenses, I had smart people on my side, all of whom supported the power of positive self-talk.

Since I had stepped off the *love train* with myself during those dark times, I figured the root of my problems was that I needed to love myself again. I knew I needed something powerful to work in my favor again.

So, I pulled out my old trick from the 90s, dusted it off, and started repeating:

"I love Me." I even pulled out my little jingle,

*"I love me. I love me. I'm wild about myself…"*

At first, it felt just as awkward as it did back then. I had to remind myself, *…it's a numbers game.*

About a month or two later, I woke up with an unexpected "directive" echoing in my mind: "Go find your joy!"

*I need to find my joy? Yeah… duh.*

*What? Where?* And this popped in my head: "The Round-Up."

*The Round-Up?! Why The Round-Up? That's the last place I'd find joy.*

The Round-Up Saloon & Dance Hall, a gay country-western bar in Dallas, was the last place I would have thought to look for my joy. I hadn't been there in years and didn't listen to or dance to country music. But this felt like "guidance" and held an energy I couldn't ignore. Like it or not, I listened.

## A Midwestern "Pretty" Boy Walks into a Country & Western Bar

That evening, I showered, put on clean underwear, and followed the nudge. As I approached the bar, I spotted a familiar face out of the corner of my eye, Mark-Brian, an old friend I hadn't seen in years. He would have walked past me if I hadn't looked to my left at that exact nanosecond. Our paths crossing felt serendipitous... and I was right.

I told him, "I'm on a quest to find my joy, and supposedly it's inside there." He laughed and said, "Let's go find it together, and I'll buy you a drink while we're at it."

We stood by the dance floor, catching up and laughing at our tragic lives—I'm not sure who won that competition. Then Mark-Brian asked me to dance.

"Oh, no. Sorry, and thank you, but *hell no!* I don't know how to country dance, and I'm not about to make a fool of myself."

He laughed and said, "No worries, I'll go get us another round."

He stepped behind me, and before I knew what was happening, he grabbed me by the belt and pulled me onto the floor. He was bigger and stronger. Locked to his hip, I had no choice but to follow his lead.

## Yee-haw Folks!

Something clicked. Within seconds, I was dancing. I'm guessing that my years of roller-dancing in the 1970s, the rhythm I gained in choir in the 1980s, and step aerobics in the 1990s came together and kicked in. Oh, did I mention Mark-Brian used to be a professional ballet dancer—he knew how to dance and apparently how to lead.

Yee-haw folks! I was dancing!

Driving home that night, as the darkness started surrounding me again, I'm not sure I had put all the pieces together, but I did recognize the freedom and joy I experienced on that dance floor. It felt like that song by Abba, "Dancing Queen," I was having the time of my life.

The following morning, as I sipped my coffee, it struck me that dancing had silenced my overthinking mind—even if it was just on that dance floor. For the first time in years, I experienced the *present moment*—and within it, joy. *OMIGOSH! I went to "find my joy"—and found it!*

## From Sepia Tone to Technicolor

Darkness filled my days, but things brightened each evening when I hit that dance floor. Because of this, I threw myself into country-western dancing, showing up nearly every night—following my joy.

I danced with anyone willing to *lead me*. I say that because after a lifetime in the starring role, I was tired of being in charge of anything. I was ready to let someone else take the lead position. It turns out that following felt like freedom. It was a lesson—possibly my first—in letting go of control.

Because of this newfound freedom as a follower, I had no desire to learn the lead position. Well, at least not at first. We'll get to that shortly.

For months, each night leaving the club, I'd drive back into my world of darkness. But even though I didn't realize it at the time, the darkness at home was slowly thinning. I'm not sure how long it took—at least several months—the fog lifted so gradually it slipped past me until one day I noticed it was mostly gone. Like when you've had a pain for weeks and suddenly realize you haven't felt it in a while. That's how it happened.

My depression lifted like magic—not overnight, not over days, but over months. Darkness was no longer my faithful companion. I know this sounds simplistic, but it wasn't. Sometimes it took a lot of effort to lift myself out of the ruins of my life and "follow my joy" each night, but I did. And amazingly, by *showing up* and *following my joy*, it worked. My fog finally lifted.

Over those months and the next several, I dropped 70+ pounds of gloom and replaced them with something lighter—self-acceptance, joy, and a whole lot of dancing. If you had told me a year earlier that I'd find my joy at a country-western bar and rise out of my darkness, I'd have thought you were high. But there I was—boots on, grinning like I'd found the meaning of life in the beats of country music songs.

I finally got how Dorothy must've felt, stepping from her sepia-toned Kansas into the Technicolor Land of Oz. My dark chapter was over—and it all started with one ridiculous little line, "I love me."

Now, I am fully aware that there are many types of depression. Mine was "situational," rooted in loss and fear. For me, following my joy was the way out—this is what worked for me—this is not the answer for everyone.

At worst, if you try using "I love me" affirmations, you might start looking up a little more often and thinking kinder thoughts about yourself. That's a start. That's something.

## Perspective and Little Gifts

This newfound joy gave me a new perspective. Living in my darkness for so long, experiencing "non-self-love and zero joy" helped me understand and appreciate a deeper meaning of love and joy once it started flowing again. Through the darkness, I gained a deeper understanding and appreciation for my light.

Dancing wasn't just about fun; it was an act of self-love. By pursuing joy, I was giving myself little gifts of love, even before I fully believed I could. These acts of love opened the door to the love I had been blocking—it had always been there, waiting for me to open the door.

That door flung open!

Yee-haw!

# I Am Ready for Love

## Drop Down, Flip it, and Reverse it

That spring and summer of 2011, I spent nearly every night dancing at The Round-Up, where my self-love and joy blossomed. I danced my ass off, made new friends, and, for the first time in decades—maybe ever— truly enjoyed my life. No dating, no hook-ups, just loving myself.

Once joy and self-love became constant in my life, it wasn't long before I wanted to share them with someone special. And that's when I got an idea. I had used my Magical Manifesting Machine for years to call forth "things," but now I would turn it toward myself and *love*. I was ready to call forth the *love of my life.*

## Calling Forth the One for Me

I've been tossing around the phrase "calling forth," so let me explain what I mean by it:

When I'm "calling forth," I set an intention, expecting it to come. Like calling my dogs inside—I don't question if it will work, I expect them to respond. OK, maybe not the best analogy, but that's how it is.

The other part to this is like tuning forks: strike one tuned to A, and a nearby fork tuned to A begins to hum—untouched. A tuning fork at any other pitch stays silent. That's resonance. This resonance is part of why we're attracted to only certain people. We are energy, vibrating, and attracting others of the same vibration—again, science. I tuned myself to love and joy—set my intent, called forth, and expected the person with the matching wavelength to answer.

All of that is to say: I was ready for love, and I called forth the love of my life.

## A New Lens

In my younger years, I built my relationships on image and looks. Every guy I dated was white. Don't hate me, but at the time, my favorite ice cream flavor was vanilla—now I love all flavors. Imagine that. Also, everyone I ever dated was around my age within a few years, and they all aligned with a superficial "type" I was attracted to at the time, mostly what I saw in fashion magazines. I was in my forties and wanted something more than physical—someone who embodied love and joy, someone who would love me simply for who I was.

## My Four Basics

I let go of my "six-foot-two, eyes-of-blue" limited thinking and opened to whoever would be an energetic match for me, regardless of age, race, or body type. I focused on *energy*. I created a list of four basics I would call forth:

1. They'd have the capacity for LOVE, as great as mine or greater.
2. They'd have the capacity for JOY, as great as mine or greater.
3. They would be "the cutest thing on the planet" to me.
4. I would be "the cutest thing on the planet" to them.

I believed that if these four elements aligned, I would win.

As you can see from numbers 3 and 4, I was beginning to understand the importance of cuteness. Superficial "looks" fade, and since I was knocking on that door of older age, I thought it best to focus on my cuteness—it grows better with age. I also wanted someone who could match my level of love and joy and possibly show me newer levels.

Despite my optimism, what some might call residual delusion, I was a walking SWIPE LEFT on any dating app. For those unaware of the dating app reference, a swipe left means you didn't make the cut.

## The Undateable Me

Here were my "stats" at the time—not exactly dateable:

- **Between jobs**—aka jobless. Can you spare $10 for a sandwich?
- **Must love dogs**—thirteen of them. Plus, one cat named George.
- **You must be okay with my roommate**—my "ex." We're basically brothers now. He lives upstairs. Totally normal. Stop judging me.

I lost most of you on the first one. The rest of you stuck around for the animals—until you hit the third and final nail in that coffin. Nobody survived that one.

Whoever it would be, they'd have to be a living saint. But powered by equal parts wild delusion and unshakable belief in how this universe works, I was filled with love and joy and knew in my heart that I'd find *the one*.

Wait. There's one person who didn't swipe left.

Is that... a line dancing Power Ranger?

# A (very gay) Country & Western Dance Hall Romance

## A Perky Power Ranger Piqued My Interest

Across the dance floor, an exuberant line-dancing red Power Ranger commanded my attention. Their energy was pure radiant joy.

No, not some random Fruit Loop geeking out in a costume at a country-and-western bar; it was Halloween weekend, 2011.

I felt a magnetic pull as their energy led me around the dance floor to gawk at them up close. I just stood there in awe, watching them do an electrifying line dance. They were wearing a full hood mask; I couldn't see their face, and the joy emanating from them exuded from their entire body.

A side note: I say "they," "them," and "their" because, with the costume and full mask, I honestly couldn't tell if this Power Ranger was a he, a she, or something more fabulous. I also couldn't see the individual's race or age.

Now, believe it or not, I'm a late-model Boomer—born the last year before Generation X. In my generation, gender-neutral pronouns weren't mainstream. I want to respect everyone, so please be patient; I'm working hard to keep up as things evolve in a more caring direction.

As I stood there, I declared, "That is the energy I want in my life." The joy emanating from them struck a magical note within me. My intention wasn't that this Power Ranger was *the one*—they represented the level of joy I wanted in whoever would be the one.

But when the mask finally came off, I saw one of the cutest thems I'd ever laid eyes on. And they were Asian, which was new for me... but exciting. This Perky Power Ranger had piqued my interest. I hadn't felt this kind of attraction, probably ever.

A month or so earlier, as I called forth the one, I had an idea that I would *feel* something when I found them. Now standing in front of this unmasked Power Ranger, I was *feeling* something.

Could this be the one?

## Meeting the Perky Power Ranger

The club was too chaotic that night to meet the person under the mask, but I trusted it would happen if we were supposed to connect. Sure enough, they were there the next time I went to The Round-Up.

I didn't hesitate to introduce myself immediately, though their thick Japanese accent and the loud music made it difficult to catch their name. After several awkward tries, I finally understood their name was Mabo. And I also found out they is a him... or are a him?

OK, my high school Honors English teacher is rolling over in her grave and kicking me in the head right now—I'm so confused. Because if they are a *he*, it'd be "he is," right? But if he is *they*, it'd be "they are"—even though they are still just one person. Now, grammar is multiplying the population. Olden-day English didn't plan for this interesting plot twist.

Either way, other than this minor confusion in my brain, I'm killing it with the pronouns, huh?

As I started asking him to dance, I quickly realized a glaring flaw in my plan: I only knew how to dance in the "follower" position. So, I awkwardly blurted out, "Do you know how to lead?" He didn't. Embarrassed and flustered, I muttered, "I guess we can't dance together," and walked away with my head down, tail between my legs. I wanted to disappear. I'm awkward around someone I like. I was extremely awkward that night.

But the very next night, Mabo approached me. He asked me to dance, and when I reminded him of our situation, he stepped onto the dance floor, offered me his hand, and said, "Let's figure it out together." A tear or two tried to pop out. How sweet is that? He placed me in the lead position and gently back-led me until I got it.

I was smitten.

## Sparks Fly on the Dance Floor

From that first dance, I felt an undeniable connection. Sparks flew— literally. I felt a tingle go from the base of my spine to the top of my head. But when I worked up the nerve to ask if he was seeing someone, my heart sank. He was three years deep into a relationship.

Still, our chemistry was palpable. Over time, Mabo revealed that his relationship wasn't quite working, which made me think I might have a chance down the line. We danced together for seven months. I fell madly in love with him; he seemed to feel the same towards me. But I crossed no lines and respected their relationship. Until...

One night, on the dance floor, he blurted out, "I love you," and sealed it with what would be considered a longer-than-friendship kiss. Mabo crossed the line, and there was no turning back. My heart sang! We began to share our feelings of love for each other, and stolen kisses when we could.

We spent more time on the outdoor balcony patio, talking, laughing, and getting to know each other.

He was still in his relationship. And I was still hopeful.

## The Literal Dance Hall Romance

We spent those seven months getting to know each other entirely at The Round-Up. You see, Mabo and his longtime boyfriend lived together and shared GPS trackers. As long as Mabo was there at The Round-Up, his boyfriend asked no questions. His boyfriend was always out playing poker and never came out dancing, so most of the dancers just assumed that Mabo and I were a couple.

We were nothing more than dance partners... who stole kisses here and there. That was it. It was innocent-ish.

It was a true (very gay) Country & Western Dance Hall Romance.

## One Honorable & Horrible Evening

One day, Mabo texted me to say he wanted to speak with me when we met that night. We always talked when we saw each other. Why was this any different? Was something up?

When he arrived at the club, he took me immediately to the outside balcony. He wasn't his perky self.

*Oh, shit!*

Something was up!

Mabo told me he needed to step back and give his relationship one last chance to see if any love existed between them. As much as I hated it, I knew this was best. It was the honorable thing to do. So, we had to stop all the kissing and professing, so he could see where they stood. How Mabo handled this made me respect and love him more—if that were possible. I told him the following so he knew where I stood:

"I'm in love with you, and I know you're in love with me. Every fiber of my being is telling me that you are the one. I'll be waiting for you if you find there's no love left in your relationship and are strong enough to let it go. I've waited 47 years for a love that feels like this, and I can wait a bit longer. But please, don't make me wait too long for that answer."

We hugged. I could barely breathe. I left for home immediately.

## Six Weeks of Hell

The weeks that followed felt like years. We still danced together, and we'd even spend time up on the balcony talking. No kissing, no professing. The conversations were more casual, more like close dance partners who loved each other but couldn't show it. I was trying to give him the space he needed, without adding any extra pressure.

It sucked!

Those weeks were dark. I'd seen the results many times with friends who had gone through similar situations. It never ended well for the outsider. I tried to hold onto the hope that it would end well, but I understood that it solely rested on Mabo and his ability to let go if there was no love left in their relationship. I figured that if he were strong enough to step away from an unhealthy relationship, that's the strength of character I would also want from the person I would share my life with.

## The Night When It All Went Down

Five weeks and six days later, Mabo's partner joined him at The Round-Up, which he never did. I gave them their space. When one of our favorite songs played, Mabo came over and asked me to dance. We usually "shadow danced" to this song, with us both facing forward and him leaning his back into my chest to follow my lead. It's a very sensual dance with my right arm around his waist, my hand on his stomach, and our left arms stretched out holding hands.

"Mabo, are you sure? He will 'see us,' and he'll know."

He replied, "This is our place—our song. Dance as if he isn't here." Once again, he stepped onto the dance floor and held out his hand. Tears welled up again.

It was like a Disney film, songbirds, lots of sparkles, and dancing rainbows swirled around us. Everything else melted away. It felt as if we were the only ones in the room. We danced like no one was watching.

Except someone was watching, and he "saw us."

As soon as Mabo stepped off the dance floor, he was escorted out the door by his partner, who didn't look pleased.

I couldn't stay at the club. At home, I couldn't sleep as I waited for a phone call, which finally came around 4 a.m.

To cut through the details and get to the good part, Mabo felt no love flowing between them. It wasn't exactly pretty, but their relationship came to an end that night. It was an extremely emotional ending.

Then he said, "I'm in love with you. I want to be with you. Can you come get me?"

By dawn's early light, he was with me.

He moved in with me and never left.

Our Country & Western Dance Hall Romance is still alive. Every weekend that we can, we go to The Round-Up and dance as if no one is watching.

## Cuteness Is Justice

Mabo moved in with me that fateful day. One year and three months later, on August 9, 2013, we got married in Provincetown, Massachusetts. Mabo has brought boundless joy and love into my life. His energy is unlike anyone I've ever met, and his motto happens to be "Cuteness is Justice." He helped me learn the importance and specialness of cuteness. I've come full circle with accepting mine.

I'm cute! And that's a wonderful thing.

Everything I called forth, including everything I thought was too much to ask, came to me in Mabo.

Our wedding, 2013.

Together, we've created a life free from drama, full of humor, and grounded in mutual respect. I've never known someone with as much joy and love. We've disagreed, but never fought, though I can annoy him greatly; however, he only holds it for about 3 minutes, never longer.

Here's my formula: I don't ask him stupid questions in the morning before he's had his coffee, or if he's busy doing something.

I've also learned that most of the time, he is right, not by default, but he's usually right. Now that I know this, I have stopped debating him on points I think are right. What does it matter?

All these years later, we still find each other the cutest thing on the planet. If I've learned anything about relationships, it's this: when you align your energy with love and joy, you attract someone who matches it. We're a match.

Mabo didn't just become my partner—he helped me unlock a level of self-love and acceptance I never thought possible. He helped me embrace my "cuteness" and love my body more.

I feel like the luckiest boy on the planet! He feels the same. But luck had nothing to do with it—self-love was the key here.

LOVE in 2025.

# In Retrospect

## Losing Every "Thing"—Gaining Everything

In losing every "thing" I thought mattered, I gained what truly does. It began with three simple words: **I love me.** That mantra sent me to "go find my joy," which led me to The Round-Up. It felt like magic—but the spark wasn't the dance floor. It was the loss.

When the life I'd built on an unhealthy ego collapsed, I dropped into the dark well that pulverized it. That contrast created clarity—the darkness defined the light. Years of feeling love's absence taught me to recognize and understand it more when it finally arrived. Stripped to my core, I rebuilt. Peace, joy, love—no longer concepts, but real. From that love, I found Mabo. Love—the everything—was there all along, I just had to lose every "thing" to see it.

The darkness defined the light. Think about it. In a brightly lit room, a beam of light might disappear. Turn off all the other lights. Now the light beam is fully defined... by the darkness. I'm thankful for that darkness.

I don't have all the answers, but I know this:

I've learned more from what I've lost than from anything I ever chased.

## Revisiting Jane & the H-Bomb Incident

Don't be too upset with Jane for doing something horrible that day at the department store when she dropped the H-bomb on this little boy's psyche.

Is it a "horrible" thing if something far greater comes of it years later?

That moment stuck. I carried body shame and self-loathing for decades, and it kept my clothes on more than I wanted. Yet it either protected me or pushed me—and eventually helped define my self-love.

I might be alive today because Jane had a bad day in the summer of 1971. In the early 80s—before we had a name for AIDS—I was old enough to be sexually active. By the mid-80s, my twenties were roaring, and that part of me wanted out. Being closeted made anonymous hookups the obvious workaround—and in those years, a risky one. It was not my virtue—I had none—but my body issues and subsequent anxiety that kept me on the sidelines and, unintentionally, safe. Thank you, Jane.

Jane's words also drove me toward a fashion degree and my first business venture—a custom-clothing business where I could design the clothing I wanted in the fabrics of my choice. This business funded the early years of my candle venture. Thank you, Jane.

The strangest-sounding gift Jane gave me was self-loathing, which defined my light. I live with a greater sense of love and respect for who I am because of this darkness. Thank you, Jane.

Because of that H-bomb moment—and the good it eventually yielded—I've stopped stamping events as "horrible" and started hunting the good in them. Over and over, I used the following line that reframed my messes:

*"I'm turning this into the best thing that could have happened for me."*

I believe Jane gave me all of this.

I can't thank you enough, Jane! You're not nearly as horrible as they all say.

### My Parents Were Moving In!

We're about to shift gears back to the story...

Thank goodness for John, my rescue dogs, and Mabo for lessons in selflessness, but I wasn't ready for what was in store for me next—guess who's coming to dinner—permanently?

# My Badass Parents

Before we jump to the day my parents moved in with us, let me rewind. If you're going to appreciate what comes next, you need to know a little more about the two stars of this part of our story—my badass parents.

## My Badass Dad

Dad with sisters Regina & Virgina (early 1940s).

## Blood in the Streets

Dad grew up in 1950s Boston, in streets paved with history—but in the 50s, they were battlegrounds for gangs, paved in blood. He lived in a war zone, caught between the Italian and Irish factions; being half-Italian and half-Irish kept him alive. He learned early on to claim whichever side wouldn't get him killed that day. Dad learned to fight in the streets.

Dad once shared this beautiful story from his childhood. When he was a small child, he remembers sitting on the curb in front of his house, watching two families go to war—a scene that could have played out in *The Godfather*. Parents, kids, and even grandparents armed with clubs, knives, chains, and meat cleavers cheered as one of the family members gutted a man right in front of Dad. My guess is that it was Granny!

"I had to lift my feet so his blood and insides could flow past me to the drain." Just another Saturday in his neighborhood.

Dad grew up watching blood and guts in the streets; I grew up watching *The Brady Bunch* on TV. Not sure which was more brutal—blood and guts, or poor Marsha taking a football to the nose.

## Combat Training—Not Just for Grown-Ups Anymore

Dad's toughness wasn't just for show; it became his skill set. On his Navy ship, he was the hand-to-hand (kill-or-be-killed) combat instructor, teaching sailors how to "neutralize" enemies in one or two moves. Basically, all Dad knew in a fighting situation ended with the other person in the morgue, and if lucky, the Critical Care Unit. He was the badass onboard—the kind of guy you didn't sneak up on unless you wanted to attend a funeral—from inside the box.

When we were kids, he turned that combat training into our family's self-defense program. There we were, a band of prepubescents learning how to "take someone out" with kill-or-be-killed tactics. Luckily, I never had to put my neutralization skills to the test. We were cute—but deadly.

Dad also believed in weight training. By high school, my older brother John David and I were the strongest kids in school, and he also held the title of "toughest." I held the title of "smart-ass."

Thanks to our prepubescent combat training, I had a delusional confidence that I could handle myself if trouble came my way. Not that I ever needed to fight—my mouth could get me out of most of the trouble it created. John David was my backup if I pushed it too far, which I did several times.

## My Biggest Cheerleader

Dad wasn't just a protector—he was a one-person cheer squad. Like me, he didn't like football, but he showed up to every game—rain, snow, or shine—shouting from the stands like I was the second coming of Babe Ruth. That's the only name in sports I know, but you get the picture.

Meanwhile, I was mostly trying not to stain my uniform. We always went for ice cream afterwards, win, lose, or draw. Blue Moon has always been my favorite flavor.

The only reasons I played football were the "cover" it provided, the quarterbacks, the tight ends, and Blue Moon ice cream with Dad.

## I Love You

Despite his rough-and-tumble past, Dad had a soft heart. He once told me he never heard the words "I love you" from his parents. It profoundly shaped him, and he ensured that we didn't grow up with the same void. He told us he loved us nearly every day, showed it in his actions, and insisted on goodbye kisses on the cheek. Even when my parents lived with us years later, if Mabo or I forgot to kiss him goodbye, he'd tell Mom, "I missed my kiss." Not bad for a kill-or-be-killed kind of guy.

## Tuesdays with Dad on Mars

Dad was always working throughout my youth; there were elderly and sick people to visit, Bible studies to attend, sermons to prepare, and sermons to deliver. However, in the summertime, Tuesdays were the day I got to spend with Dad on his errands.

My favorite stop, and the only thing about our Tuesdays I remember, was going to the post office, where inside was a candy shop where I could choose three pieces. Snickers, Milky Way, and Peanut M&Ms were my favorites. Interestingly, Mars, Inc. was the maker of all three.

I guess I'm a Mars kind of guy.

Looking back, with a wife, five kids, and a congregation to focus upon, Dad's time was limited, but these Tuesdays with him made me feel loved and special. They were enough. I'm sure Mars had something to do with it.

## So, That's Where I Got It

I think I now understand that my tendency to overshare came from Dad. I never realized it until after Mom died, but looking back, Dad was an avid oversharer, like me. And like me, some of his stories were simply horrifying.

One morning at a Denny's while on our road trip after Mom died, out of the blue, he blurted, "You know, Jim, before your mother, I had fast cars and faster women." I dropped my fork. "Oh, jeez, Dad! Why would you say that? Nobody needs that image burned into their psyche. Please, don't ever repeat that to anyone."

Instead, I just now put it into print—available worldwide. Now, who's the bigger oversharer? He taught me well.

## From Bad Boy to Bible Boy

His journey from streetwise rebel to ultra-conservative preacher is legendary. That last story now gives this one more street cred. When he met Mom, her mother laid down the law. No marriage would be allowed unless he converted to their faith. Smitten, Dad dove into Bible studies.

He nearly got kicked out before he even started his first lesson. Dad tossed the preacher a beer and offered him a cigarette when he first showed up at his place. Luckily, the preacher tossed it back and gave Dad a free pass.

However, he quickly adapted to his new ultra-conservative lifestyle, and not only did he convert, but he also became passionate about it, attended college, and became a full-time minister. No more drinking, smoking, or anything "faster" for Dad.

Dad's worldly background made him relatable and non-judgmental. His sermons focused on love and forgiveness instead of fire and brimstone.

Near the end of his career, when he was preaching at a smaller church, the Eldership demanded he preach out against homosexuality on a Sunday I was visiting; I was completely out by then. Dad preached on unconditional love instead. He was "let go" for "undisclosed reasons." That's a badass Rock Star move on Dad's behalf!

### Dad to the Rescue

Growing up, I thought Dad was at least somewhat homophobic, based on things he said when gay characters popped up on TV. However, more recently, he shared a couple of stories that completely reframed my perspective.

Without a prompt, Dad jumped into a story from aboard his ship in the Navy. "A couple of men were caught 'in the act,' and a group of guys were going to toss them overboard..." That caught my attention! "...and I don't mean for a nice swim!" He paused. "And... and?" I prompted.

"Well, I stepped between them." "And?" "I told them if anyone laid a hand on these two men or said anything further, they wouldn't wake up to see tomorrow." He commanded such respect that nobody dared say or do anything to harm them. He ended up protecting several other guys as well. He admitted he didn't understand sexual feelings between two men, but he saw their humanity and the danger they faced.

I sat there, stunned—mouth open. I had never heard that story before.

He continued, again without a prompt. "As a boy, I was targeted by several predators. I fought them off. I learned early on how to take care of myself. It scared me, but nobody ever messed with me."

I flashed back to the comments I remembered hearing him say when I was younger. It was never about gay people being gay. Each of those TV programs was about predators preying upon innocents. Dad was not homophobic; he was against anyone hurting or preying upon others.

Dad showed me his character through his actions on that ship and his love for his two gay boys.

I realize Dad and I share the same nurturing instinct and empathy for the underdog and the vulnerable. Even as a young sailor, he instinctively protected and showed kindness, not judgment. That's beautiful.

That's my Dad—the badass.

## My Badass Mom

Mom's upbringing wasn't as dramatic and colorful as Dad's—no blood-filled streets, no kill-or-be-killed combat training—but she was a badass in her own right.

Mom was born in Denver and raised by her mother and grandmother. Her father took off shortly after her birth. Decades later, she discovered she had eleven step-siblings from several different moms. If that wasn't exciting enough, both grandparents on her Dad's side were 100% Native American—Powhatan. Mom wished she could have learned more about her heritage. Me too.

As a kid, Mom competed in horseback riding and was an excellent violinist, but she never did either again after becoming a mom. Her mother was a tall, self-sufficient German woman; her grandmother was a tiny, wrinkled dynamo who smoked like a chimney. Mom would sneak cigarettes into the bathroom and smoke with the window cracked open. Her grandmother smoked in the house anyway, so no one was the wiser.

Mom, the rebel without any possible cause. She got her twisted sense of humor from her grandmother; her mom was more serious.

### Flash, Flair, and False Eyelashes

Mom liked a little flash and had a lot of flair—rhinestone pins, false lashes, and a hint of Beautiful by Estée Lauder that lingered in the hallway after she passed through. She was always a sharp dresser, and until her final months, she wore full makeup, false eyelashes, and beautifully coiffed wigs and wiglets.

Her looks made a statement, but her strength didn't need to—it was steady, quiet, and always in the room, like good lighting. She lived with a glimmer of light and a hint of mischief in her eyes.

### Some Funny Shit

Mom wasn't one to swear very often—her only go-to was "SHIT!" And that was seldom. She'd work herself up, fists shaking by her head, before she could let it fly. "SHIT!" As kids, we'd scatter, laughing hysterically.

In her later years, while living with me, I once pushed her limits. One day, after teasing her relentlessly, she finally broke.

There she sat in her Barcalounger—eighty years old, full face of makeup, false eyelashes, one always a bit wonky, and a perfectly coiffed wig slightly askew from napping—when she turned to me and spat out the now-infamous words:

"Jimmy, you're such an... ass!"

I nearly peed, I couldn't stop laughing. For both of us, that was a big moment. I wore that first legitimate swear word like a badge of honor, another one to add to my Scouting uniform. The "Ass" badge.

## Working That Runway & My Lady's Dress

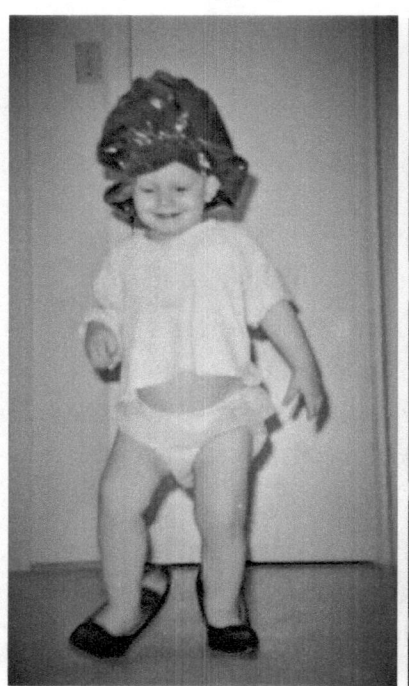
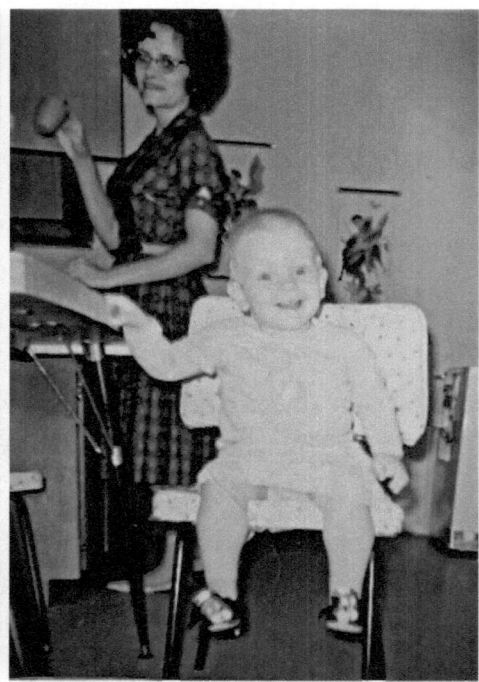

When I was a toddler, Mom let me run around the house in her high heels and shower cap. And was proud enough to take photos.

Then they bought me a light blue nightgown—just long enough for me to call it my "lady's dress." I wore that lady's dress until it was a crop top. Somehow, Mom never had a clue what was to come.

## Bedtime Back Scratches

Every night before bed, usually while watching TV, I'd curl up next to Mom, hunched forward like a cat begging for attention while her perfect-for-back-scratching nails did their thing. I also got them nearly every night they lived with us. I think I miss that most—nobody's nails ever came close to Mom's. They were tiny magic rakes that could scratch every worry right off my shoulders.

## My Lighthouse

Her badassery was subtle but profound. She loved fiercely, yet softly and unconditionally, even at the risk of losing everything they had worked for. In her final years, when she lived with me, she showed me patience, kindness, and humor in the face of circumstances truly unimaginable. She was my lighthouse—and still is.

Thanks, Mom, for being the badass we all needed.

If I thought Mom and Dad were badasses back then, they had more in store for me after they moved in. We'll get to that soon enough.

That's enough to paint the picture.

Now, let's continue... reset the scene:

And just when I thought I finally had my shit together as far as compassion and selflessness, the ante got upped.

My parents moved in with us.

Cowboy Dad & My Beautiful Mom, 2017

# Three Gays, Preacher & His Wife—One Roof!

BREAKING NEWS: *"On July 12, 2016, at precisely 2 p.m., a preacher and his wife from an ultra-conservative religion moved in with their gay son, his husband, and his 'ex,' also reported to be a male. Analysts predict turbulence. Stay tuned for further developments."*

Yes, it was true: my parents moved in with Mabo and me, along with my ex-partner, John, and four dogs. But there was no drama.

Mom thought she'd won the lottery, and Dad wanted a cowboy hat, now that he was a Texan. The only drama was that he wanted cowboy boots, but with his questionable walking skills, no boots for Dad.

John and I have shared this house since the mid-90s. Now, John and his husband live two hours away on a lake, but our house is John's "in-town" home during the week, closer to his work.

He and I have become like brothers; we would do anything for each other, and we share a brotherly love. But like brothers, we don't need to spend too much time together. We hardly ever see him coming or going. He stays upstairs in his "apartment" and doesn't share the downstairs with us. We no longer bicker like we did those first few years after the breakup. Somehow, it just works.

The miracle in this arrangement is that there's never been a cross word or thought between John and Mabo. Mabo accepts John as my brother, and they get along fabulously. Mabo has inherited an incredible wardrobe, as John has outgrown it—sweet deal for Mabo.

As for our animal family, we were down to only four dogs at the time. The original 13 Dogs and a cat named George now live in Doggie & Kitty Heaven... waiting for me. By the way, I've chosen to go to Doggie & Kitty Heaven, it sounds like more fun.

So there we were, the preacher and his wife, their gay son, his husband, and his ex, all living together with four dogs in what could have been the perfect setting for lots of drama—it was anything but.

My parents adored Mabo and John, and their feelings were mutual. This situation may be challenging for some people to believe, but it actually worked quite well. There was no judgment, just love and gratitude. Growing up in Japan, Mabo was used to multi-generational households; both sets of his grandparents lived in his family home. John has a deep appreciation for family, and he was 100% on board when I first mentioned them living there.

## Mabo's Citizenship

Soon after my parents moved in, Mabo became a citizen. My parents were thrilled and so happy for him. We also honored Dad as a veteran. Mabo's mom, in Japan, knitted these American flag bow ties, including one for Dad. What an incredible day!

What we lacked in drama, we made up for with hilarious stories, especially about Dad—always the unintentional star of his own sitcom. Since he didn't have a sense of humor, he never realized how funny he was. Here are a couple of examples.

## The Case of the Chocolate Chip Cookie Dough Bandit

When my parents moved in, we set up their own living space in our home, complete with all their furniture. They had everything they needed to feel at home, and apparently, Dad felt extremely at home.

It was the peak of a Texas summer, and I kept the thermostat at a sensible 80 degrees to save on electricity. I also figured all old folks like it hot—Mom, yes, but Dad, I learned, not so much.

I walked into their room one day, as was usual. Mom was sitting there with a blanket pulled up to her neck, and there was Dad, sitting in his La-Z-Boy, looking content as ever. His shorts were neatly folded across his lap, which seemed odd. But then, below the shorts, something caught my eye.

*Is that chocolate chip cookie dough?*

As I got closer, I saw that what I thought was actual cookie dough was, in fact, Dad's *cookie dough*. He was naked from the waist down. What appeared to be chocolate chips were broken-up pieces of pleather from his decaying La-Z-Boy stuck to… can I stop now? This is making me sick.

"Oh, JEEZ! Dad! What the hell? Put all that away!"

"You've got it so damn hot in here, Jim, I had to do something to cool down. I didn't know what else to do!"

"Well, Dad, what you could do, at the very least, is put a towel underneath what's going on down there! This is so wrong on so many levels of wrongness! You can't un-see this sort of thing!"

Mom, who hadn't noticed Dad's solution for ventilation, chimed in. "John! That's disgusting! Put your pants on! Nobody needs to see that!"

"Well, Mom, there's probably a market for this sort of thing on the interwebs." I had to speak their language. "So, Dad, want to set up a 'Fans' page? We could name you The Cookie Dough Bandit."

"Jim, why would I want to start selling cookies?"

"Maybe—to make some money for my soon-to-be therapist?"

"I haven't baked in years, Jim!"

"...but there you are with your goodies proudly on display. OK. Let's drop this and get you a new chair."

We replaced the La-Z-Boy with a Barcalounger-Lift model, added a washable cover, and kept the A/C set at a chilling 70 degrees for the rest of the summer. It was worth every penny.

I'll never be able to look another chocolate chip cookie in the face again without reliving this tale. However, it won't stop me.

## Guessing, Aiming, and Helmets

We also gave my parents a pristine 2007 Prius to maintain their independence. However, only Mom was allowed to drive it after we experienced a harrowing ride with Dad behind the wheel during their final months in Michigan, before they moved down to Texas.

On a short trip from their apartment to Costco with Dad behind the wheel, Mabo and I rode in the backseat, white-knuckling the ceiling handles, because our lives actually depended on it, on the longest 10-minute drive of our lives. Here's a snippet from the audio of the ride:

"Dad! You almost just clipped that car! DAD! What are you doing?!"

"Blinker! Use your BLINKER!"

"NO! Not the freeway! God help us!" As he crossed all four lanes without a glance, going 27 MPH. Surrounding us was a cacophony of honking, hands in the air, and fingers flying, as they shouted "WTF?!" With Dad casually drifting between the lanes.

"Pick a lane, Oh, JEEZ! Dad! Pick ONE LANE!"

"The gas pedal is on the RIGHT—you're going 38 MILES AN HOUR—on the FREEWAY!

"Mom, why do you let him drive?!"

Dad replied for her, "I wouldn't call it driving, Jim. It's more like I'm just guessing and aiming at this point."

"Then AIM for the EXIT! Blinker... use your... this is ridiculous! When you move to Texas, you're not driving anymore!"

"But Jim, my doctor said I have the reflexes of a 20-year-old."

"Tell that to your feet, Dad. Tell that to your feet."

Picture Tim Conway's old man shuffle—Tim would win Dad in a race.

### Mom and Her Racing Stripes

Mom's driving wasn't much better. Within the first few weeks, she added embossed "racing stripes" down both sides of our once-pristine 2007 Prius. After the first "stripe," I asked, "Why didn't you stop when you first heard the car scraping something, and turn out away from it?" She shrugged nonchalantly and said, "Well, Jim, I got nervous and decided to keep going."

One day, they came home with a scratch on the roof—*on the roof!*

"Mom, how did you manage a scratch down the length of the roof?"

"I don't have a clue how that one happened."

"Neither do I, Mom. I have no clue. We'll wait for the next scrape before we fix them. Maybe they'll give us the old-lady-multi-scratch discount."

"That seems like a good idea, Jim." Not an ounce of shame.

I made them wear safety helmets on their outings from then on.

## Love, Laughter, and Helmets

Despite the driving mishaps and the Cookie Dough "situation," having my parents live with us went surprisingly well. Their presence enriched our lives in countless ways. Yes, Dad drove me a little bananas because he was used to being in charge and happy to assert it in every situation. But we managed, and it helped that he constantly, and I mean constantly, thanked me for taking such good care of them. It's hard to stay frustrated with someone who is endlessly thanking you.

They reminded me that family isn't about racing stripes or cookie dough but love, laughter, and adapting to whatever life throws at you, even if that means replacing recliners and making your parents wear safety helmets while they drive around town. I should have gotten bumper guards to surround the car—and the roof!

## It Was No Accident

Some might think I accidentally left out my parents' names this whole time. I didn't. To me, they are simply Mom and Dad. I never called them by their names unless I was filling out a form for them or trying to get their attention in a crowded store.

For the record, to the outside world, if it matters to you, they're known as John and Judy.

And John and Judy, the preacher and his wife, were about to become "rebels with the greatest cause" and go down in the history books. Well, at least in this history book.

# A Preacher & His Wife Walk into a Gay Bar

## Yes, This Happened

Mom's love was so pure and consistent that it was easy to miss—like air, it was always present, always necessary, and often unnoticed until something monumental took your breath away. One such moment came shortly after my parents moved in with us in 2016, when Mom made a request that stunned me.

"Jim, when can we go with you to The Round-Up? We'd love to see where you met Mabo and watch you two dance."

*Wait, what?! My parents—at a gay bar?! Watching me and Mabo dance?! Without wheels?! Did I hear that correctly? Did someone dim the lights? Am I having a stroke?*

"Mom, are you serious? You do know that The Round-Up is a gay bar, right? A gay bar—gay people *dancing* with other gay people in a bar that serves *alcohol* to *gay people*. Are you sure about this?"

Mom smiled, her eyes sparkling. "Of course, I know where you met. Don't be funny."

"And Dad—what about him? Does he know you want to do this?"

"Yes, you goofball. He's excited, too. Now, when are we going?"

My parents. At a gay bar. Watching me, their favorite child, and his husband twirling on a dance floor. My heart smiled with a fluttering ventricle. I wasn't sure if this was a good idea or a recipe for disaster.

Mom had one request: no social media. She didn't want to have to explain this "outing" to her ultra-conservative friends. Fair enough. So, under a cloak of social media silence, we planned their visit for a quiet weeknight when the bar would be less crowded, and our friends would be there to meet them.

## A Front Row Seat

We set up a table at the edge of the dance floor, giving my parents a front-row seat. Our friends gathered around to meet them.

When it came time to dance, Dad pointed at his cane sitting on top of the table like it was a weapon of mass destruction and winked. "Go have fun, fellas. I've got you covered." And yes, in Dad's hands, that cane was a lethal weapon of protection—even in his eighties.

This was shortly after the Pulse Nightclub shooting, and Dad was always concerned for our safety each time we left the house to go dancing. That night, Dad had our backs, just in case anything happened.

Mabo and I stepped onto the floor and danced to several songs. As we twirled around, I saw Mom wiping tears from her face. She glowed, and her eyes sparkled.

When we returned to the table, Dad repeatedly said, "Congratulations, guys! Great job out there!" "Dad, it wasn't a competition... but thank you." "Congratulations!" he replied.

Earlier in the book, I mentioned that the Three No-Nos from my ultra-conservative upbringing would play a pivotal role in shaping my relationship with my parents, "though perhaps not in the way you'd expect." Well—ta-da! Consider the loop closed:

*Mom and Dad in a gay bar, surrounded by two-stepping cowboys watching their son dancing with his husband, with unconditional love in their hearts, and Dad standing guard to protect us.*

You didn't see that one coming, did you?

Neither did I.

## A Seismic Shift in Love

That night, lying in bed and reliving the evening, a realization struck like a lightning bolt.

For over sixty years, an ultra-conservative faith had shaped my parents' world—a world where dancing, drinking, and homosexuality weren't just frowned upon; they were "mortal sins." Yet there they sat, at their request, in full approval, with love in their hearts.

This action was anything but tiny. This was a tectonic shift, a seismic realignment that had to have been decades in the making.

Yet, their decision to join us at The Round-Up didn't feel like a stretch or a compromise to their values. It felt natural, comfortable, and precisely as it should be.

Many years ago, all of this would have been unthinkable and a non-probability. I now have a greater understanding of what unconditional love looks and feels like.

## The Grandest Expression of Unconditional Love Imaginable

This story wasn't about rejecting their faith or turning their backs on their beliefs. Above all else, it was about embracing the absolute power of unconditional love. Their presence at that gay bar, watching their son and his husband dance, was the most profound expression of love and respect they could have ever shown us.

Now, after Mom's passing, the memory of that night has only grown in significance. It stands as a testament to their understanding that love, pure, unconditional love, is what truly matters most.

My parents are rebels in the best possible way. Rebels with a cause. They didn't just step outside the comfort zone of their younger lives—they shattered it, lit the pieces on fire, and made s'mores—and enjoyed them.

I don't just love them for it—I stand in reverence and ahhh.

Life in the House of Belasco was running so peacefully, so beautifully—better than I ever imagined...

But wait... who's that knocking at the door?

# Knock, Knock—Who's There?

### The End. The End, Who? The End is Near!

All was well—until it wasn't. For nearly four wonderful years, my parents were in good health and enjoyed their independence, driving everywhere they needed to go. Each year, they flew to Florida to stay with friends and Susan for a month or two—until COVID-19 hit the fan in 2020.

Nothing was the same.

Despite masking, hunkering down, and practically bathing everything in Peroxide, COVID eventually came knocking. Like idiots, we opened the door. A health worker, unaware they were sick, came to the house. We all got sick.

It was rough, but we all made it through. However, in Mom's case, just barely—though, even that's debatable.

She already had scar tissue in her lungs from a previous illness, making COVID especially dangerous. Twice, we had to take her to the hospital. Watching her get wheeled through the ER doors, knowing I couldn't go with her, was soul-crushing. Did I mention *twice*? The image of her fearful eyes behind that oxygen mask still haunts me.

It now tops my list of "things I wish I could unsee." At least it finally knocked Dad's infamous cookie-dough incident out of the #1 spot.

Seriously, though, having my parents' survival in my hands was already terrifying. Then Mom got some more bad news, the worst kind.

## Mom, Me & the Apocalypse

Just as Mom began recovering from COVID, things took a turn—so did I.

In early 2021, in the middle of the global pandemic, we found out she had cancer. Due to her current health status, she was too fragile even to consider any of the treatments for this type of cancer. Her prognosis? Three to six months.

She handled it with remarkable grace. I, on the other hand, did not. I was already teetering on the edge of despair—this was the Apocalypse.

Living through COVID with my parents' lives squarely on my shoulders felt like starring in a mash-up of *Raiders of the Lost Ark* and *Groundhog Day*. Except in the scene where Indiana Jones sprints for his life from that giant boulder, I'm getting flattened—and it replays daily on a loop.

Now, with Mom's cancer diagnosis blended with COVID, throw the movie *Doomsday* into that mash-up.

Seriously, lightness aside, I felt hopelessness again, the first time since my Dark Period, only this one was darker—this was Mom.

My everything.

## Sucker Punch!

The cancer diagnosis that shattered me? It wasn't just bad—it was the worst-case scenario, kind of bad. Bone marrow cancer. Multiple Myeloma. The kind of diagnosis that comes with hushed voices, time limits, and a horrifying endgame.

The options were... not really options.

The endgame? If she lived too long, her bones would become so brittle that the pressure of a hug—or a shift in bed—could snap them. Mom was an angel—what kind of mercy is that?

The word "suffering" hung like a black cloud between my ears. But Mom didn't flinch. She wasn't having it. Determined, she was not going to allow cancer to take her life. Atta girl, Mom!

The Oncologist alerted us that any of the cancer treatments would end her life sooner, and she would be miserable; she was too fragile from her previous illness—let's not say that name again. So, that, coupled with the horrible endgame of this cancer, was the only thing we were looking to do: strengthen her bones. Her doctor got approval to use an osteoporosis medication to stabilize her bones. It worked—one treatment was enough. Hallelujah!

They gave her six months to live, tops. Mom stayed a year, and with no major pains and not one broken bone.

During that year, each of the Belasco kids made the trek down to our house in Dallas and spent time with her; some made multiple trips. It was beautiful.

Cancer didn't take her life. When her body had had enough, and she was ready to go, miraculously, she got a UTI, coupled with Pneumonia (that we didn't know about). The combination made her go to sleep and pass two days later, in peace and no pain. That's the most Mom thing I've ever seen.

## A Final Sparkle & Confirmation

Mom's eyes always carried this glimmer of mischief and joy. It was constant, unwavering, and somehow unshaken, even in her most challenging moments. But she gave me a gift in her final moments—a sparkle I'll carry forever.

She had been asleep for two days, her body preparing for its final goodbye, and was now in her hospice bed. She lay quietly, Dad holding her hand, as I kept kissing her forehead and saying, "I love you, Mom," hoping that she might hear me and know she wasn't alone.

At one point, Dad handed me a napkin to wipe my tears away. After a good wipe down, I realized it was one of the old, greasy ones he kept under his ball cap. I almost threw up. Dad chuckled. Now he finds his sense of humor?

Suddenly, she opened her eyes.

I launched onto the bed, leaning into her line of sight like an eager puppy. At first, her eyes were gray and distant, like she was looking through me. But then, her eyes focused. The hazel color returned.

Her face came alive with a flash of recognition and a smile.

It wasn't just her usual glimmer. It was a radiant sparkle—just for a moment—before she gently closed her eyes for the last time.

*She saw me! SHE SAW ME! Ah... she saw me.*

In that flash, neither of us was alone—and we both knew it.

That's all I needed.

The pain in my heart melted. Peace settled in.

Her final gift calmed my greatest fear—of losing the first and most significant love of my life.

She gave me her final sparkle, as if finally giving me confirmation of something I always believed. So, respectfully, to all my siblings, let the records show:

I am Mom's favorite.

## The Sunshine in Mom's Soul

I'm forever an optimist, and didn't think those two days of sleep would be her last, so when the morning call came from the hospital—"Come immediately!"—the others had no time to fly in. All the kids and her best friends called in to say goodbye, hoping she could hear them.

Dad and I were at her side, my sister, Susan, singing hymns on the phone with Dad joining in, beautifully off-key, as usual. I couldn't speak, let alone sing. Around the time of "There Is Sunshine in My Soul Today"— one of Mom's favorites—she stepped off the train and into the sunshine.

She was there for my first breath, and I was there for her last.

# Peaceful Delight

## It Just Popped Out

While writing this book and describing how Mom lived her life, I was typing in my usual stream-of-consciousness blur when these words landed on the page:

Mom lived in a state of peacefulness, with a sense of delight...

*peaceful delight.*

I'd never used that term before, but it fit so perfectly that I now treat it as a formal title in her honor, Peaceful Delight.

She didn't just live with Peaceful Delight—she embodied it.

Just sitting across the table from me, sipping coffee. She was it.

Mom had a curious, almost playfully mischievous, look about her. Looking back, she almost always had this glimmer in her eye and a smile on her face, like "What trouble can we get into next?"

Some of my earliest memories were at our house in Rochester, NY. I would have been around five. She would smile really big and say something like, "Let's go see what we can find today!" I was thrilled to embark on another adventure with her, as she grabbed my hand and headed towards the stream behind our house. I remember watching tiny little fish swimming. One day, we saw a frog. I cried. That one scared me.

Every day that she lived with us, even during our (my) Apocalypse, knowing her end was near, she'd look up at me from her Barcalounger, with a sparkle in her eyes and a jingle in her words, "What kind of trouble can we get into today?" She was the calm within my storm.

## Living It Together

I wish I could say I was able to share that Peaceful Delight with Mom during her final years, but I was incapable. Part of me wishes I could return, be more present, and live within that energy alongside her.

Since she passed, in subtle and not-so-subtle ways, I'm constantly reminded that she's living it with me every step of the way.

Jimmy the Elf & Mom, Christmas 2019.

# Learning, Then Drowning in "Selflessness"

### Rescue Animals & Mabo to the Rescue

As has been clear throughout this story, before learning to care for others, I teetered between Self-Attention Surplus and Self-Absorption Syndrome. My shift toward selflessness began with John's love for animals and, by extension, for me.

When we rescued our first animals, something stirred within me: compassion and a sense of selflessness. These helpless creatures needed love and attention, and I felt it flow outward from me toward them; of course, it was always flowing back from them. They became like my children, softening my heart. I needed them as much as they needed me.

That compassion grew stronger when Mabo entered my life; something shifted again. More than ever, I wanted to share my love, my space, and even the last scoop of ice cream with someone other than myself. Mabo's love made me want to look outward.

Over time, my selflessness expanded beyond my family to include others; I stopped being so selfish and became a more balanced, functional human being.

## Burnout in Disguise

Those early years with my rescue animals and Mabo were just the warm-up act. Then my parents moved in, and Mom's health collapsed. At first, my selflessness seemed balanced. But as things grew darker for Mom's prognosis, my grasp on selflessness collapsed as I fell into the deep end without a life jacket. I poured everything into keeping her afloat—and there was nothing left holding me above the surface.

Apparently, I wasn't listening at the beginning of every flight I've ever taken:

*"Put your own mask on first before assisting others."*

Instead, I floored it—blew past the exit for Selflessness—and drove straight into Self-Sacrifice.

Maybe if I'd taken the right exit, I could've been more present with Mom—really enjoyed our last months together—instead of being completely out of my mind. If I have one regret, it's this.

On a phone call with a close family friend, they said, "It's a noble thing taking care of your parents, but especially for what you are doing for your Mom..." But it didn't feel noble. It felt like drowning. What I thought was love was really self-neglect in disguise.

At the time, I told myself I was practicing love. But looking back, I see now I wasn't. I was drowning in the idea of selflessness—giving everything away without giving anything back to myself so I could be there more fully for her. That's not unconditional love. Love doesn't flow in one direction only. It flows in and out. I just hadn't learned that yet. For so many years, I had the flow going one way in; now it flowed one way out.

## The Toll

By the end, my mind, body, and spirit weren't even on speaking terms. Three anxiety meds to get through the day, workouts long gone, meals grabbed from whatever landed closest to my mouth. Lifting Mom constantly created issues in my shoulders, elbows, and locked up my hips, leaving me walking like Frankenstein's sad cousin. It took a year of physical therapy after she died to walk normally again without pain.

The anxiety left its own calling card—my hands shook nonstop. They still do, just less. Medication helps, but the issue persists. Now I see it as proof I made it through something awful—not the end of the world, as I once thought.

In that final year, I tried to hide it all, so Mom wouldn't feel worse than she already did. But she knew. She always knew.

I wasn't there for myself, but she was there for me. She always was.

Mom, Dad, and Mabo became the life raft I couldn't build for myself. They kept me afloat when I didn't have the strength. I wasn't a graceful passenger, but they carried me anyway—and I'll be forever grateful.

# Just One Tic Tac Away

## Crazy? Yup!

In March of 2022, after two years of quarantine, keeping Mom alive, and helping her through her death, I was one Tic Tac away from roller-skating down 8th Avenue in NYC—against traffic—dressed as a roller-derby chick.

Oh, wait—that actually happened years prior.

This self-indulgent pause is here solely so I can tell you this story and pretend there's a lesson in there somewhere. It also felt like time for some levity after the last several chapters.

Here's the story:

On Halloween 2002, one year after 9/11, Michael Todd, our friend Tom, and I roller-skated through NYC dressed as roller derby chicks, Tina, Rita & Maudie. Michael Todd's Tina looked like she woke up on her doorstep, Tom's Rita was a devil-child, and I was the chubby "pretty" one. Typecasting.

Some might say we were a bit "out of our minds" as we skated against oncoming traffic down 8th Avenue, but we made thousands of people laugh when they needed it most. Cars pulled over to snap a photo. Eventually, a traffic cop waved us over—we thought we were getting a ticket—but he wanted a photo instead.

It was pure joy.

But joy wasn't the point. I told you I was going to pretend to squeeze a lesson out of this, though it's more of a point.

The point is: as half-out-of-our-minds as that NYC adventure sounds, by the time Mom died, my mind had entirely departed. I needed to escape that house before the world around me hated me.

## Speaking of (nearly) Hating Me

A few days after Mom passed, Geri Ann came to help sort through Mom's things. She is one of the sweetest humans alive. Apparently, I was being "a complete ass!" Geri Ann's words, and she doesn't usually swear. I guess Mom was right.

A couple of months later, when I regained my humanity, I apologized. Geri Ann said, "Well, thank you. I wasn't sure if I wanted to speak with you again." And honestly? I don't blame her.

And of course, I'm her favorite sibling again.

I didn't just need fresh air—I needed freedom. Freedom from that house. Freedom from anyone needing anything from me.

Forrest Gump, move over. Jimmy needs some space and time to heal. From what? I don't know!

*Just get me the flip out of this flapping house!*

# Run Jimmy Run!

## A Little Bit Psycho

A couple of weeks after Mom died in March 2022, I looked at Mabo, trying to keep my voice calm and my hands from twitching.

"I need to drive. A road trip to... nowhere," I said. "Now. Before things get... Norman."

He gave me his infamous side-eye—the one that said, "Do I ask, or just help him pack his bags?"

"As in Bates," I clarified. "Norman Bates... *Psycho*—the movie?"

All I got was a blank and confused stare.

The only part he clearly understood was the word *psycho*—as it related to my condition—and he wasn't disagreeing. He was fully on board now.

I wasn't planning on murdering anyone. But I also knew that if I stayed in that house for one more second, I might start wearing my mother's dress and wig and rock myself into skeleton form. (movie reference)

Mabo quickly replied,

"Take your dad with you... Please. Take all the time you need."

So much was packed into that "Please," it was palpable.

Mabo bolted for the suitcases. In less than an hour—to be exact, fifty-three minutes—he had everything Dad and I needed packed into the car and ready to go.

As he was buckling Dad into the passenger seat, who was still wondering if he was getting dinner, a second thought hit me.

[*Psycho* soundtrack, cue the violins.]

"But... Mabo... a road trip with Dad? Are you sure this is a good idea?"

(Spending an undetermined number of days trapped in a car with the Commander-in-Chief sounded like a highly probable disaster—or, at the very least, a one-way ticket to me "assisting" Dad into oncoming traffic.)

"Best idea I've heard in years, no turning back now!" Mabo said, kissing us goodbye. "Good luck, everybody... especially you, Dad!"

That was the fastest "idea to execution" I've ever had.

Thank you, Mabo!

### All Aboard! The Gang's All Here

Mom came along for the ride—in both ash and spirit. Mabo joined us as a puppet. Yes, we have puppets of ourselves—because, of course, we do.

Muppet-Mabo held Mom's urn in his arms, safely buckled in the center backseat so that I could keep an eye on them in my rearview mirror.

## Something was Missing

A few days into the trip, I noticed something was missing. Not my filter or any ability to stop overthinking—I never had those.

It was Dad.

No, I hadn't "accidentally" left him at a rest stop, and no, I didn't "assist" him into oncoming traffic. What I realized was missing was Dad's Commander-in-Chief-ness.

## The Unexpected Joyride

To my surprise, and Dad's good fortune, the trip was going quite smoothly. Dad, for the first time, just sat back and enjoyed the ride. Whatever I wanted to do, he was game. His usual command mode was gone. Not only did I not need to redeem that one-way ticket for Dad, but we even started "cycling" together—as in syncing up bathroom breaks, mealtimes, and just about everything.

*Omigosh! I am my dad. This wasn't the oneness I was asking for.*

As the miles progressed, Dad was just my dad, not the one trying to run the show. I realized that in the past, whenever Dad's "Commander-in-Chief" mode was in high gear, it was always centered on Mom's care and comfort.

When they lived with us—especially during the thick of her illness—it felt like living with a one-person command center. Every day, every night— without fail—came the orders.

My usual response?

"Dad! Have I ever—once—forgotten to pull Mom's blanket up to her chin, put on the blue socks instead of the pink ones, or set her water on the left and the phone on the right? And for crying out loud, you really don't have to remind me to turn out the light every single night!"

He'd just smile and say, "Thank you for all you do for us, Jim. Don't forget to hit the lights on your way out. Goodnight."

Petty things, really—yet in the throes of my apocalyptic meltdown, it drove me bananas.

I felt like such a jerk after misjudging him for so many years. It lasted about ten miles. "Oh, look, Dad! A Dairy Queen—next exit!"

"That sounds good, Jim."

I no longer had a Commander-in-Chief riding next to me; what remained was just Dad. A human being. Quirky, surprisingly chill, full of appreciation, and old stories I'd somehow never heard.

## I'm So Confused

One such story is about him proposing to Mom on the first date. Did I mention, first date? It had all the makings of a beautiful romance—except for the part near the end where he used another woman's name.

"Dad! Who's Trixie?! I thought this was a story about Mom!? Are you telling me I almost grew up with a mom named Trixie? Was she a stripper or something?"

"Well, Jim, I think I'm confused. That story might not be about your mom. But then again, it might. Either way, I married your mom. Who cares how we got there?"

## Just Dad

By the end of that leg of the trip with Dad, I saw him in a new way. Not just as my oversharing dad, but as someone I genuinely liked. Someone I respected.

Someone I'd miss once the passenger seat was empty.

# The Road Trip

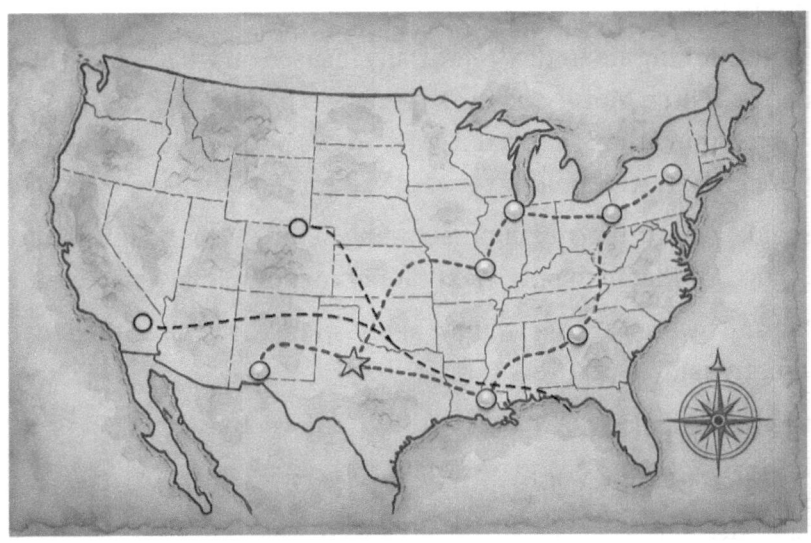

Map(-ish)—for entertainment purposes only.

On the first leg of my six-month odyssey, Dad and I first drove to Michigan. (Map not accurate.) At the top of our list was one of Mom's dearest friends, who was in the ICU recovering from heart surgery. We grew up with her family, and she was like a second mother to me.

Out of respect for her and her family's privacy, I'll refer to her as Mom #2 to keep the story straight. Mom #2 was the person my mom spoke to on the phone nearly every night before going to bed.

Over the years, both Moms lived through many illnesses and scary times, using up most of their Nine Lives. Mom hit her limit first, but Mom #2 had made it through yet another one. I hadn't seen her in years, and despite her current heart situation, she looked great that day.

What makes this next part so special is that Mom #2 was more conservative in her thinking about my "lifestyle," or, as I might call it, my "orientation." Her opinions on this subject were no secret.

But what Mom #2 and I may have lacked in shared life views, we made up for in shared love for Mom. Through this love, we became friends.

In those last several years, we had many wonderful phone conversations. It felt like we shared a respect, which is wild, considering the vast chasm on certain topics between us.

Without thinking about it, we naturally focused on what we had in common—at first, Mom—and from there, it expanded. We found more common ground than I expected. I'm sure we both felt it. We made each other laugh. I started looking forward to our talks; I believe she did too.

That said, I was firm in my understanding of how Mom #2 felt about me being gay. So what happened next caught me completely off guard.

As Dad and I were packing to leave her hospital room, she called me over and quietly said,

"I owe you an apology."

*Wait—did she use the A-word?*

"For... what?"

Her eyes filled with something tender as she took a breath and continued.

"Over the years, I've judged you harshly for the way you lived your life."

Then she said something that would echo in my heart for months—and eventually inspire this book:

"Your mom's love for you—and your love in return—softened my heart and changed my mind."

I stopped breathing as she continued.

"Your mother showed me what unconditional love looks like."

All I could do was mouth the words, "Thank you."

I didn't realize it at the time, but her words planted a seed that would change everything for me. They would also be our last goodbye.

She used up her ninth life several weeks later.

## Unconditional Love & Mom

As Dad and I continued our journey, we visited the church where we grew up, the same place where he spent much of his career preaching. The moment we walked in, I could feel Mom's presence lingering in the hearts of everyone there. I found out that's not just a figure of speech.

One after another, people approached me, eager to share how Mom's unconditional love had shaped their lives. Unconditional love—that phrase kept popping up over and over.

*Was she handing it out like candy?* I thought I was the only one.

Some told stories of her simple kindness—small gestures that had left a mark decades later. Others, now grown with families of their own, said she made them feel like one of her children. More than a few even swore she made them feel like they were one of her favorites.

*Hold on, slow down, everyone—that's my title.*

But what really threw me was the sheer number of kids who lived with us. One after another, people said they had lived with us, and not just for a night or two, but for months—long enough to call our house "home."

I smiled and nodded, but inside I was puzzled. I remembered kids staying with us now and then, sure—but not most of the ones who stood before me that day. Back then, we Belasco kids weren't told why these kids just showed up, and, truth be told, I still didn't know.

It left me with one more question for Dad—something to talk about on our long drive back to Texas.

As we traveled the country, staying with family friends along the way, the phrase "unconditional love" kept coming up when we discussed Mom. At this point in the trip, it had to be dozens of people using the same term to describe her.

Mom wasn't just generous with her love—she was unconditional. She had an uncanny ability to see people, really see them, and love them exactly as they were, in ways they so desperately needed. Mom made everyone feel special, not just me. I gained another level of admiration.

"Unconditional love & Mom"—this followed me.

## There's Always Room for One More

On our trip back to Dallas at the end of April 2022, I asked Dad about all the kids from our church who had lived with us.

"Well, Jim, when their parents were going through a rough spot—divorce, addiction, fighting, whatever it was—the kids often ended up at our door. Sometimes they showed up with a suitcase, sometimes with nothing. Most stayed for weeks, one stayed for about a year."

We lived in a house under 1,000 square feet. I bunked in the basement with my older brother and sister, and by the time I left for college, I probably missed a lot of the kids who stayed with us. However, I still didn't remember so many kids living with us.

Dad was not a preacher who made millions. He was a poor, honest preacher, with five kids and whoever else happened to show up.

"With all the kids left on our doorstep, how did you manage to feed us all? I know how much—or little—you made."

"I never worried about it," he said, "somehow, there was always enough."

"How come you never told us what was going on?"

"It was none of your business. What was going on in those people's lives was nobody's business."

"Well, did they at least give you money to help feed them?"

"No," he said flatly. "That wasn't a thing back then. We all just helped each other out."

The truth is, I never once heard my parents complain. They never gossiped, never argued, never even let on how tight money really was.

Looking back, I don't know how they thought they could take in other people's kids with five of their own and no extra money.

But somehow, they did.

## Powdered Milk & Government Cheese

And now that I think about it—maybe I should've known. We drank powdered milk every morning. For you young ones, or those lucky enough to grow up with real milk, that's dehydrated milk powder that's mixed with warm water. The dry, unmixed clumps would detonate in a chalky sludge in your mouth. It was disgusting. And no, I never got used to it. We were so poor that the poor people from our church dropped off their government cheese. I remember loving that cheese. I didn't know better.

We always had enough.

I didn't even know we were poor—not until I grew up.

## There is Always Enough Love

Mom and Dad never ran out of love. They were proof that love doesn't ration itself. It stretches. It multiplies.

For years, I hoarded love, as if it might run out. I remember thinking I needed to hold onto my love so I wouldn't run out.

Somewhere between Mom and Dad's open-door policy, the animals John and I rescued, Mabo's love, and those grueling years of caregiving, it finally clicked:

The source doesn't run dry—it's like a water hose attached to an endless river. I just have to stop pinching the hose.

And the ones who modeled this weren't saints or self-help gurus.

It was Mom and Dad, running a family of five plus an unofficial orphanage with a revolving door, saying,

"Come on in, there's always room for one more."

# A Gift, A Note, and a Little Red Bird

## Dad's Gift

In early May 2022, when Dad and I got home to Dallas, my older sister, Geri Ann, flew in to care for Dad, giving Mabo and me a chance to take a well-deserved vacation together. Of course, it was another road trip—because why stop now? Where? Florida, to go roller-coaster hopping—something we love to do and have done all over the country.

When Mabo and I returned, Geri Ann had "news." Dad wanted to move back to Michigan to be closer to family and friends. Dad told me, "I want you to have your life back after giving yours up for us."

Oddly enough, even though it was a huge gift, it felt like another rug pulled out from under me. I had already accepted that I would continue my role as Dad's caregiver.

What was I thinking? Of course, this was the best move for Dad and me—once I thought about it. Dad would be closer to more family and friends, and I would get a chance to regain my life. Geri Ann and Susan had already prepared everything for Dad's new living arrangements, and he needed to be there within the week to secure his spot at the assisted living facility.

The complex where Dad wanted to move had a special connection—it was built decades earlier with funds he had helped raise. He knew people who lived there and people who ran the place, so this was a good fit for him, and most importantly, it was where he wanted to live.

With no time to waste, we packed as many of his belongings as possible into my car and took another road trip back to Michigan. Once there, my siblings took over his care, officially relieving me of my duties. The shift felt strange—like I'd lost a part of myself—but I was deeply grateful.

With Dad settled, I could finally "find myself."

"Could someone please pass the milk carton?"

I needed to find out where I was last seen.

## A Note from The Great Beyond

I missed Mom terribly—her voice, her laugh, the feel of her nails scratching my back before bed, and our morning coffee-time together. All the little rituals I'd taken for granted left an aching void.

That first morning back in Dallas after dropping Dad off in Michigan, the emptiness felt sharp. Mabo was at work, and I stood in the kitchen, lost in the quiet. As I reached for the coffee maker, something caught my eye—a small note stuck to the fridge with two mismatched magnets.

It was about two inches by four, smudged with what looked like spaghetti sauce, and written in Mom's unmistakable handwriting from before her illness. I froze. I don't remember ever seeing it, nor does Mabo when I asked him later. It had to have been there for at least three years, hiding in plain sight—quietly biding its time—until that moment.

Her voice came through so clearly, especially that middle line:

*I may not be there for coffee, but I will be there in spirit.*

I burst into tears. I hadn't cried since the day we said goodbye. These tears were different. I knew I wasn't alone.

Just like her final sparkle calmed me, the void I'd been carrying since her passing felt full again.

Yes, I still miss her voice, her touch, her laugh—but my grief loosened. My memories of her became beautiful again.

*Mom is with me in spirit.*

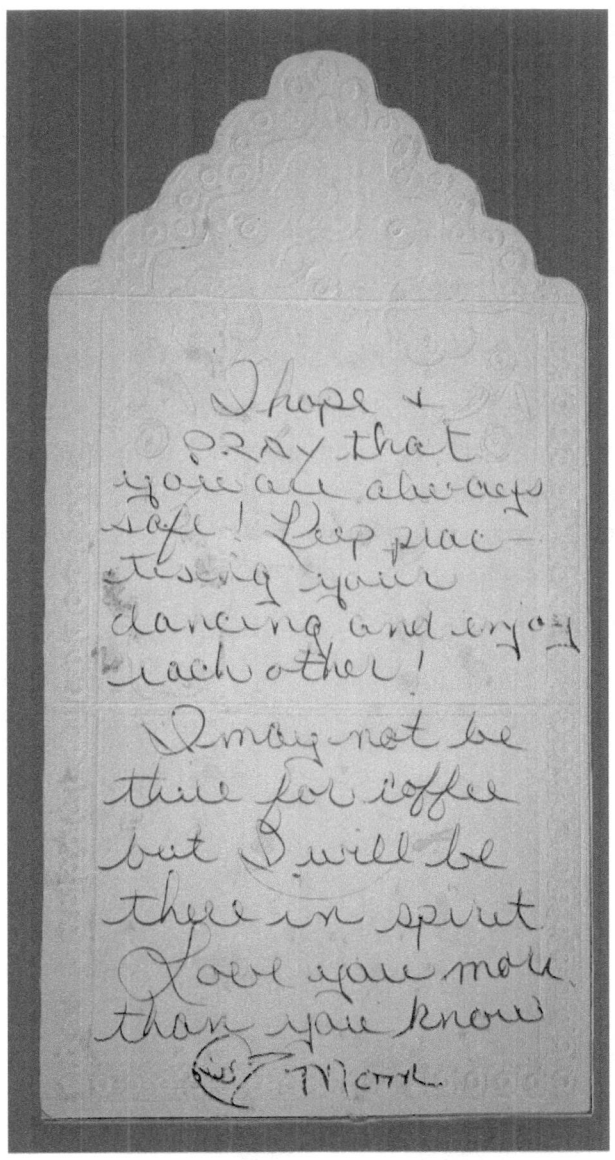

*I hope and PRAY that you are always safe!*
*Keep practicing your dancing and enjoy each other!*
*I may not be there for coffee, but I will be there in spirit*
*Love you more than you know*
*Mom*

## So, Now What?

As I sat in the kitchen with my coffee that morning, for the first time in years, I thought about myself.

And it scared the absolute hell out of me.

*What in the world am I going to do now?*

## A Little Red Bird that Wouldn't Shut Up!

On a side note, when I returned from my six-month road trip, a little red bird started tapping on our bedroom window, on my side of the bed, every morning. Like clockwork, around the time Mom used to wake me up to start the day, it was tapping away. It felt like Mom was annoying me awake, just like when I was a kid.

"OK, Mom. I got it. Good morning. I'm up! Stop it already!"

I hated it and loved it simultaneously. This bird was persistent, continuing for months, until one day it suddenly stopped.

Strangely, I was OK with that. I knew Mom was still with me.

# Mirror, Mirror, on the… What the Hell?

### Who Am I?

One morning, shortly after Mom's coffee note, I found myself standing naked in front of the mirror, taking stock of the damage for the first time in years. I planned to ask myself the classic existential question, "Who am I?" But what came out instead as I looked at myself was:

"Who am—who—what… who the HELL IS THAT?"

*That can't possibly be me. Could it?*

*Oh, Jeez!*

My silhouette had morphed into a "silhou-WHAT?" I looked like the Pillsbury Doughboy if he'd made all of life's wrong choices. It wasn't just my body—it was everything. I had no idea who I was anymore.

*OK, Jimmy. Let's not ask too many questions right now. And for goodness' sake, keep your clothes on—one battle at a time.*

Guess what was in store for me next?

Taking my clothes off in front of people!

And I did it.

# Me? A Nude Male Model?

### Husky Dreams Do Come True

It was probably the end of May 2022 when I got home from dropping off Dad in Michigan, and I "received" that note from Mom. Being alone in that house while Mabo was working was not good for my mind. I must have had a form of PTSD with that house. I had only been home for a few days, and the walls were closing in on me. I had to get back on the road—my mind was fixated on that idea.

That's when I received the call that would make my road trip possible. My Magical Manifesting Machine must have been listening. It was my sister, Susan.

"Hey, Susan, what's up?"

"How would you like to meet me all across the country this summer and into the fall? I need a scan model, about your age and size, though, technically, you should be a little bit bigger."

"Can I drive my car? I really need to drive more, I'm not done."

"Done with what?"

"Never mind. Does it pay?"

Susan worked for a company that sold the latest mobile ultrasound device for heart scanning. Her job was teaching technicians nationwide how to use it properly. To train her students in real-life situations, she needed "scan models." She was looking for a man over 50 who was on the heavier side.

Hmmm.

*Drive across the country by myself?* Check.

*Meet up with and hang out with my sister?* Check.

*Get paid for it?* Double check.

And the cherry on top...

*Eat with free abandon?* Check! Check! Check!

Then she mentioned that I would need to take off my shirt during the scan. I was desperate for the road and very hungry, so I'd take one for the team. I couldn't raise my hand fast enough!

"Susan, you're a lifesaver! Thank you!"

"Pack your bags, I need you in Ohio next week."

*Hell, yes! Call me Poppin' Fresh! Pass me the fried chicken, ice cream, and maybe a side of pie to keep things balanced. I'm hitting the road again!*

Suppose my HUSKY little seven-year-old self could see me then. I was a partially nude plus-size model where chubby was a requirement.

Finally, HUSKY had a job description that didn't include the word shame.

And yes, Mabo was very supportive of this extension of my road trip.

He kept saying, "Take all the time you need... Please."

## The Road Paved with Mashed Potatoes and Gravy

This gig was more than just a paid adventure. It allowed me to reconnect with myself in a way I hadn't expected. The miles alone, the time spent with Susan, and the laughter were everything I needed.

I'd lived in the darkness, this most recent time, for over two years and had forgotten what it felt like to find joy in the simple act of living. And if that joy came with an extra side of mashed potatoes and gravy, so be it.

I needed this as if my life depended on it!

## Cinnamon Rolls are Magical

Behind ice cream of any kind, cinnamon rolls are my second-favorite food group. Traditional, fancy, iced or not, with or without pecans—even the ones raised and glazed to resemble a donut—I love cinnamon rolls.

I'm not entirely sure why I felt the need to share that, except that they were a favorite staple of my modeling gigs that summer and fall.

Those hours behind the wheel gave me joy, but they also gave me space to reflect on Mom's love and its incredible ripple effect. Look at the effect it had on Mom #2: my Mom's actions softened her heart and changed her mind.

Mom was unaware of the dozens of people whose lives she had deeply touched.

Mom was amazing. And she didn't even know it.

What she did in her life was nothing short of revolutionary. She changed the world around her, and the worlds of those around them, and so on, and so on.

And to pull this section full circle, which has nothing to do with cinnamon rolls, that ripple effect—oddly enough, is shaped very similarly to a cinnamon roll with pecans and icing.

Don't try to figure it out. I'm just hungry.

# Nothing Groundbreaking Here

## Printed on T-shirts Since the First Cave Person

The lessons I was about to learn, which we're about to cover in the following chapters, weren't new, groundbreaking, or complex. Honestly, they were embarrassingly basic. What puzzled me most wasn't the lessons themselves—it was how spectacularly I'd managed to avoid their meaning for over half a century.

You've probably heard all of this before. I'd also heard all of this before, and look where it got me—driving all over the nation with a stupid grin on my face looking for marbles.

Here's the strange part: what I was about to learn from Mom on this trip felt revolutionary—earth-shattering, even. But none of it was. All of this probably dates back to the first cavepeople. There's nothing new under the sun—except for this self-proclaimed expert in avoidance finally paying attention.

And once I did? My life quietly, beautifully, became something worth loving.

Now, this might sound a tad dramatic, but don't forget my state of mind just before this road trip started, right after Mom died. You might have found me curled up in the fetal position, gnawing on my arm hair, mumbling something about being a boy and not a dog. Serenity? Yeah, I'm pretty sure that's not what it looks like.

So, how does one go from arm-hair-gnawing despair to discovering the key to a life worth loving? Great question. I thought you'd never ask.

The answer begins here—with a thump to the back of my head.

# A Guideline for Humanity?

## A Familiar Thump

A couple of weeks later, on my drive from that first gig in Ohio to the next one somewhere in the south, a question was rolling around in there. I remember the exact moment I asked it out loud, because I was driving across that spectacular bridge on I-40 that crosses the Mississippi River from Memphis into Arkansas.

## Question #1

This question turned out to be the first of several that spring, the answers to which would blow my mind and heart wide open.

Mom's unconditional love had become something I fixated on since the first week of my road trip, and I couldn't figure out how she did it, and for so many people. I wanted to be more like Mom.

**"OK, how do I become unconditional love?"**

Almost instantly, with a flick to the back of my skull, right behind my right ear, a phrase I was familiar with popped into my head:

***"Treat people the way you want people to treat you."***

It's not what popped in my head, but the tap to the back of my head that had me puzzled. Weird stuff like this occurs in my world all the time. The puzzling part was that the tap felt like one of those *thumps* I'd get from Mom when I sat in the pew in front of her and wasn't paying attention in church. I know her thump well.

*OK, something is going on here.*

Now, the phrase that popped into my mind was one I'd heard plenty of times. It was The Golden Rule, sans the King James Version "thou's" and "thy's." Yet, another odd thing—it was Mom's wording, the way she would say it to me as a kid, so I'd understand it. Although I'm not sure if I heard her voice when this happened, right now I can see and hear her saying it—in those exact words.

**"Treat people the way you want people to treat you."**

I thought I knew that rule, but out of curiosity, I Googled it like I do nearly everything. What I found stunned me. Again, forgive me for nerding out; I love learning the history of stuff like this. And this "rule" has some history.

That message has shown up in nearly every civilization with written records. The oldest known version dates to Egypt's Middle Kingdom— centuries before it appeared in any religious texts. It's a guiding principle across cultures, belief systems, and eras.

It seems to be one of humanity's few shared truths, a guideline for all humanity.

From what I gathered, it all boils down to empathy, reciprocity, and compassion.

Was this one of the original Universal Guidelines for Humanity?

## The Wallpaper of My Youth

Growing up as a preacher's kid, I'd heard "Love thy neighbor as thyself" and "Treat others as you wish to be treated" so often that they faded into background noise. The Golden Rule was everywhere—embroidered on doilies, framed on walls, stitched into pillows. It was the wallpaper of my youth, right next to needlepoint Jesuses and cross-stitched reminders to "Count Your Blessings."

Embarrassingly, until this moment of "discovery," the Golden Rule held about as much weight as the kindly restroom reminder:

*If you sprinkle when you tinkle, be a sweetie and wipe the seatie.*

It had been staring me in the face all these years, and I didn't see it. I'm now referring to the Golden Rule, not the "sprinkle when you tinkle" guideline for toilet etiquette.

"Treating people as you want people to treat you," in one form or another, seems to have been around since the beginning of, well, humanity.

### Dad, Did You Know This?

Loaded with my "discoveries," I had to call Dad.

"Dad, did you know that..."

Of course he did.

Dad shared this; it was so simple and clear:

"If you live your life through the lens of love, you're golden.

That's the greatest act you can do."

I was a preacher's kid. I should've known this stuff!

Seriously, I'm not sure how I never ended up on the side of a milk carton.

### So, How Do I Become Unconditional Love?

Apparently, it's simple.

Don't be a jerk.

Well, there's probably a little more to it, but this is a good start.

### My #1 Goal

Not long after this epiphany, I wrapped up my bare-chested modeling gig in the south and headed to the East Coast—the Carolinas. I heard myself say it aloud—like the words had been waiting for me to say them:

**"My #1 goal is to love unconditionally, like Mom."**

The weight of that didn't crush me—it felt natural. I didn't know what loving unconditionally would look like for me. I didn't know what it would cost me—or how it might save me. But something inside wanted this.

I had no idea what I'd signed up for—but life would be my teacher. And I was starting to think that the flick behind my ear was from Mom, tossing me one of her pearls.

## If Penguins Do It—Why Can't I?

I was driving through Asheville, and it was majestic—naturally, that made me think of penguins. The connection? They were Emperor Penguins. They're majestic.

As I considered how empathy, reciprocity, and compassion would be essential for any civilization's survival, I recalled a documentary about Emperor Penguins in Antarctica.

The penguins huddle together to survive brutal winters, with temperatures dropping to -58°F and wind speeds hitting 124 mph. That is damn cold and damn windy. Those on the freezing outer edges take turns moving to the warm center, and those in the center rotate outward to the edge, where some of them die. They do this instinctively—because the colony's survival depends on it.

The penguins' huddle demonstrates nature's "don't be a jerk" clause in action. Each individual makes sacrifices for the greater good.

I'm no penguin expert, and I'm not saying penguins can feel empathy or compassion, but it seems evident that this kind of mutual care is part of their DNA. It got me thinking that it must be in my DNA, too.

Perhaps the issue is that I have too many options—and keep choosing myself over others.

I can't promise I always took my fair share of turns at life's cold outer edges. But I have the power to choose differently.

It's already in me. I have to choose it.

And being the kind of human I wish others would be to me?

That might be the greatest thing I could ever do.

# Mom's Pearls

Consensus Was—It was Mom

On the Fourth of July weekend in 2022, I visited my friends, Tami and Donald, in Tennessee. I'd been traveling the past couple of months and was ready for a break. That weekend, we circled one topic again and again—that first pearl. That pearl had been rolling around in my head since it hit me weeks before. The consensus was—it was Mom's.

When I left their place, questions started popping up like road signs demanding my attention. I was chasing clarity on my newly declared quest to be unconditional love, like Mom.

*Loving myself?* I didn't need to ask that one; it's obvious. I could eat better, exercise more, and maybe stop inhaling quite so many burgers on this road trip. *Whoa, slow down, Trigger, we're moving a bit too fast.* I wasn't ready for that level of commitment. *Baby steps.*

*Loving others?* Now, that was where I thought I had it all figured out. I've always considered myself a loving person—I'd never deliberately hurt anyone. *Surely, I'm nailing this one.*

## Question #2

With a gut feeling that Mom was the one who threw that first pearl, I had a half-hearted question for her. This question was laced with sarcasm because I thought I had this one in the bag:

**"How could I possibly improve upon loving others?"**

On cue, it hit me—SMACK—another, what we're now calling pearls, to the back of my head.

It was as if I heard Mom's voice this time:

*"Get serious. You're not done yet, Jim. Keep going. Keep asking."*

She called me "Jim!" I knew it! There are only three people who call me Jim, and the other two are still alive and not answering questions in my head. *Thank goodness it's not my overactive imagination—those are Mom's pearls.*

So, I started asking the questions as they came, trusting she'd lob more pearls my way. I put on my proverbial catcher's glove and helmet for the pearls and got started.

"OK, Mom, I apologize. I'll take it seriously. You have my full attention!"

## Question #3

With some reflection on my track record of self-absorption, which mysteriously popped into my head, this next question felt like a solid starting point. Honestly, I was still a bit fuzzy about how I might be failing in the "loving others equally" department.

**"In what way am I not loving others?"**

This pearl hit me like a "you should know better" thump. It came in the form of a memory from a few years before, during a heated conversation with someone I deeply love, but with whom I deeply disagreed. The topic? Politics. Yeah, I know better now.

As the debate bubbled dangerously close to a boil, I abruptly shut it down:

"OK, let's stop talking now before I start hating you!"

I was "joking"—and 100% serious. I couldn't fathom how anyone of sound mind could be that stupid. This person's "soundness of mind" was seriously in question even then, as I was remembering it.

Incoming! Boom! Another pearl hit without me asking a question. Evidently, I wasn't getting the point of the first one. It landed with one simple word:

*"Judgment."*

*Who? Me? I'm the least judgmental person I knooo... oooh... I get it.*

Yep, I couldn't finish yet another sentence, even if it was just to myself. There it was—full self-realization, delivered with all the subtlety of a cast-iron skillet to the back of my head:

*I'm judging others for their politics... and probably much more.*

The irony stung. I loathed others' judgment, yet I found myself judging others daily.

*Gotcha. OK, something to work on.*

And with that realization came the most natural follow-up question.

## Question #4

**"What is the source of these judgments?"**

This one felt like a brick to the head. Again, the answer came immediately, in two words I really didn't want to hear:

*"Cable News."*

*Wait! Not my friends!*

They kept me up on all that was going wrong in the world—and all the possible scenarios that could go wrong next—backed by a panel of experts giving their opinions. Surely, they weren't the problem!

I realized I had let these so-called "friends" spoon-feed me more than just "news." The reality is, there wasn't much of any "news" at all in that diet. I had willingly followed them down a rabbit hole into a fantastical world of opinions and probabilities disguised as truths. I let them shape my worldview—and, worse, they helped me form my judgments of others.

Looking back, during an election cycle, COVID, and cancer, my "friends" weren't informing me; they were fueling my anxiety, harsh judgments, and hopelessness. I had enough on my plate without their diet of fear.

It doesn't matter which side of the political coin you land on. These cable "news" stations are serving *fear* on a silver platter. The more we fear, the more we watch, and the more we fear. Repeat.

When I finally disconnected from cable news, I realized what I'd been consuming wasn't bringing out the best in me. It was quite the opposite. I'd been feeding my fear, not my love.

That was a wake-up call.

## Question #5

Part of my hopelessness was actually a sense of helplessness. I felt helpless. I felt powerless to make changes in this ridiculous, mixed-up world. So, this became my next question:

**"What can I do to change the world besides voting and visualizing whirled peas?"**

This pearl came in the form of a Gandhi quote. Mom and I watched a film about him during the pandemic. We discussed this topic a lot.

*"Be the change you wish to see in the world."*

Ah, yes, there it was.

I just needed a reminder to *be the love I wish to see in the world.*

Then, Mom #2 popped into my head, and a flood of all the people I crossed paths with that spring, all touched by Mom's love.

Mom's unconditional love changed the world—starting with the world around her and spreading outward in ripples. *Beautiful.* I just smiled.

This strategy seemed a much more effective way to change the world than sitting in silent, and not-so-silent judgment of others, thinking I knew better than everyone else, and becoming increasingly upset and fearful about it each day.

In my past, I chose, for some strange reason, to spend time judging others and being mad, upset, and frustrated all the time. It took a lot of energy to be me—especially trying to keep it silent. There I was in my Apocalypse, not changing anything but increasing my heart rate and anxiety pill dosages.

Now I know—that was my choice. What was I thinking? I wasn't.

Nowhere in any theology, school of thought, or cave wall drawing does it say, "Judge your neighbor." *Oops!*

## Question #6

Most of all in that moment, I wanted peace. My mind seemed to be what I was trying to escape. For many years, I constantly thought about everything that could go wrong—on an endless loop. I didn't use to be like this.

**"How can I create more peace in my life?"**

POP!

*"What are you feeding yourself?"*

I already knew this—maybe I just needed the reminder. What I ingest shapes me. Not only what I eat and drink, but what I watch, listen to, think about, and visualize—not to mention who I surround myself with—all contribute to who I am and the energy I carry and send out.

Not only had I been binge-watching Netflix, which isn't necessarily a bad thing, unless you go too deep into the *Tiger King* series, but I was also bingeing on Fear TV. Then, I'd listen to friends go on and on about all the world's problems and why we should hate certain people for causing them. After that, I'd watch all of it get rehashed and escalated all day long on the "news," all while I'm watching my most lovingly favorite person in the world slowly die, step by step, before my eyes. It was too much. And I was absorbing it all... at my will.

*Maybe if I had limited what I was ingesting during Mom's illness, I could have been there for her more.*

Right on cue, my grandmother's voice (Dad's mom) delivered one of her favorite gems:

*"If you hang around shit, you begin to smell like it.*

*Hang around it long enough—you become it."*

Thanks, Nana. I remember it well.

We loved it when she came to visit. There was a lot of cussing and always some liquor hidden in the top cabinet. John David and I would stand on the countertops to look at it. John David was smart enough to try it once. Of course, he got caught. He got the old:

"This is going to hurt you more than it hurts me." Or something like that.

To the best of my recollection, the timing of questions #2-#6 fell rather closely in sequence. It may have taken about a couple of days. I remember the questions and the answers clearly; the details surrounding them are a bit fuzzy. Once I got into it, it was like being in the zone.

Those were the key questions up to that point; let's continue down the highway on this little road trip.

# That's a Tall Order!

My Impossible Dream?

As I traveled the country that summer and into the fall, I found myself sharing with others what I'd been learning from my dear, dead Mom, along with my goal:

*To find love in everything and everyone, including myself, and to treat people the way I wanted people to treat me.*

Surprisingly, nearly every person responded the same way, though their phrasing varied:

"Wow. That's a tall order!"

"I can't. I hate people!"

"Who do you think you are, young man, Jesus Christ?"

The consensus was clear: my goal seemed impossible—or, at the very least, wildly unrealistic.

This series of overwhelming reactions threw me a bit. I'd been doing it—or at least thought I was—and it didn't seem insurmountable.

*Am I fooling myself?*

Over the miles, as more people piped in on my latest pipe dream, they all agreed—"That's impossible." Doubt started to creep in. Maybe this was too high a bar, even for me. Could we truly "just be love" and "love everyone" in this messy, conflicted world?

## Question #7

I finally threw another question out there for Mom:

**"How can I love everyone in these times? This feels too big!"**

KABLAM! A bowling-ball-sized pearl, rolled right down the lane. STRIKE!

*"Love is..."*

I expected something profound or new, but instead I heard something old. Familiar.

I know this.

"Love is patient. Love is kind."

I stopped after the first two of a longer list.

*Patience?*

*Kindness?*

*The TOP TWO definitions of love?*

*Hmmm.*

Two more words that had lost their meaning for me. They always sounded like the word equivalent of cotton candy: super sweet, with lots of fluff, but little substance.

*Can loving others and myself be as easy as practicing patience and kindness?*

(This question might qualify as #7.5)

*Noooo...*

POW! BAM! SNAP! CRACKLE & POP! (Brain-synapse connecting.)

*Patience and Kindness are LOVE!*

*I can do that!*

*That's achievable!*

*If I can't be more patient and kinder to myself and others, I need a heart transplant!*

## Mama Tried, and May Have Finally Landed a Big One

Apparently, I don't have to be Jesus, Buddha, or Mr. Rogers to start loving others. All I need is some patience and kindness.

I remember my mom trying to teach me about compassion, patience, and kindness—words I could never quite grasp.

As a kid, I understood *compassion* as "suffering with someone." I remember those words precisely. The idea wasn't exactly at the top of my list. Extra suffering? I was too busy trying to hide a ten-ton rainbow colored elephant named Nellie in my closet. I already had a full-time job.

What I missed is that the "suffering" part means to *feel their pain*—empathy. That changes things a bit. But I was learning that there's another side to compassion: the action part —the outward choice to care—to do something. And guess what that action part is?

Patience and kindness.

*Well, well, well. I'm finally learning the inner workings of compassion.* Of course, I looked all of this stuff up, and, wouldn't you know, love in the form of compassion, empathy, and kindness has also been baked into humanity all along—fancy that.

## The Universal PSA for All Mankind

Humor me again; I'll keep it brief. In my research on compassion, patience, and kindness, the oldest information I found dates to ancient Egypt, around 2800 BCE. They had a concept called *Ma 'at*—showing up with compassion and integrity, which at its core reflects patience and kindness.

Centuries later, it appears in Vedic texts as *dayā*, "compassion toward others."

Centuries later, Buddhism and the Hebrew Bible/Old Testament began using the term *loving-kindness*. Centuries later, the New Testament carried it forward. There's its beauty.

The Universal PSA for *all humankind* is:

**"Please be patient, please be kind."**

## Beat That, Mr. Grinch

All of this is what Mom had been trying to teach me all along.

Love isn't a tall order.

It's as simple as:

Patience and kindness.

Simply, love in action.

My heart grew to ten sizes that day.

Beat that, Mr. Grinch.

Thanks, Mom.

*Wait! Hold on! What about THEM?*

## Loving the Unlovables?

It took about five minutes after my big victory dance with the ten-times oversized heart when this hit me:

*How can I love someone I don't even like?*

Some people make it impossible to like, let alone love, them.

Some might call them "the unlovables." We all know at least one. I think I've been on a few people's short list.

I cannot walk around pretending to like everyone—that's not going to happen.

## Question #8

**"OK, Mom—how am I supposed to love someone I don't even like?"**

POP! This one tickled and made me chuckle.

*"You don't have to like someone, agree with them, or even know them to show them patience and kindness. By doing so, you're loving them."*

That, my friends, was music to my ears!

## I Don't Have to Like You to Love You!

I drove around with an even bigger dumb-ass grin on my face on this one! This answer from Mom was the cherry on top of my double-decker hot fudge sundae with whipped cream and roasted pecans.

The more I thought about my newest realization, the more I smiled.

Here's where my head is on this:

"Liking everyone" and "loving everyone" both sound impossible—one of them, I'm convinced, really is impossible.

I realized that liking someone is a matter of preference. Comfort. Chemistry. It's emotional and subjective, and usually involves shared values. You know—stuff you can't force.

It's not realistic for me to expect to like everyone, and I don't think it's possible. Some people seem impossible to like, and no amount of *kumbaya* is going to change that.

I used to think loving others had to come with a warm feeling attached, and if I didn't like someone, there was no way I could love them. But I see now that loving someone doesn't require me to agree with them, or feel any spark of friendship at all.

It's me choosing, in that moment, to respond with patience, kindness, and respect—not with lashing out, indifference, or judgment.

And once I started looking at it this way, the impossible suddenly became possible. I don't have to like everyone. Thank Goodness! But I can love them. I can choose to treat them the way I want to be treated, even if we disagree, even if we're on opposite sides of everything, including the planet.

That shift changed everything for me.

Liking has limits. But love has no limit.

And nowhere does it say that we must *like* our neighbor.

*I'm loving this!*

## I've Got Options

Here's what I finally realized: I've got options.

I can put the Universal PSA into practice and show patience and kindness to people I don't know, disagree with, or flat-out don't like.

I can mind my own business—this saves everyone a lot of frustration and sounds like an act of kindness to everyone, including me. You know what else is none of my business? What other people think or say about me— they own that one. Another round of kindness... on me!

And when other people stick their noses in my business? Here is where I get to practice patience.

I also realized that loving others wasn't an insurmountable task; it begins with showing myself patience and kindness. I can do that.

When I started with myself, it naturally spread to others, whether I liked them or not.

The reward? A kinder, more loving world—for everyone, including me.

# "I'm Done."

It was late in the fall of 2022, as I pulled into my driveway after my final half-naked modeling gig, something struck me. Just like the end of Forrest Gump's cross-country cathartic run, my own cathartic road trip across America had come to a close.

*That's it. I'm done.*

And that was that.

The part of me I was searching for?

I think I found him and much more—hidden somewhere inside those pearls.

Now, I just had to deal with the aftermath—namely, the 20-plus pounds of "joy" I packed on along the way.

Damn those cinnamon rolls. But I enjoyed every twist and turn.

## Eight (or so) Questions

Roughly eight key questions, and I received a lifetime of answers.

In those six months, I learned more from Mom than in the five decades prior.

Now, it was up to me to put all I had learned into practice.

# Me, a Ride-Share Driver?

After a few weeks' break from my six-month road trip, a friend suggested I try driving for a ride-share service. I love people, talking, and driving—so why not?

I ended up enjoying it even more than I expected. Part of why I enjoyed it was that I didn't work evenings or nights. I can promise you that the first passenger to have thrown up in my car would have been my last.

No, I stuck to afternoon riders—people just getting around town on their day. Strangely, despite over 5,000 rides, my life was never threatened, and I was never treated poorly once. By the way, those are the top questions asked, besides, "Who was your strangest rider?"

Each ride became a chance to practice patience and kindness. I'd greet riders with a smile, use their names, check their comfort level, and ask about the music. Nearly everyone thanked me as if I'd offered them a luxury service instead of a basic courtesy. It shocked me how many riders said that most drivers didn't even bother to say Hi.

The bar was low, so a clean car, good music, safe driving, and a little human kindness went a long way. Their gratitude came back to me in smiles, five-star ratings, tips, and, surprisingly, even hugs. Yes, hugs.

### Have You Ever Asked Your Ride-Share Driver for a Hug?

Over time, my car turned into a rolling confessional, a sit-down comedy club, and therapy sessions—me as the "therapist!" I imparted my old-man wisdom to countless younger people who asked some rather deep questions.

One afternoon, a woman climbed in after getting "dumped" by her boyfriend, right there on the sidewalk.

It wasn't a pretty sight, and I was relieved when he stayed there, and only she got into my car. After listening to her story, we had another form of therapy; we spent the remaining 30 minutes of her ride singing along with her favorite songs and laughing that man right out of her head.

When we pulled up to her stop, she grinned and said, "Best breakup ride ever!" Then she asked for a hug. Of course, I got out and gave her a big hug. As I drove away, I wondered, *How many breakup rides has this poor woman had?*

She wasn't the only one who asked for a hug; I lost count. All were women, except for one man whose hug stuck with me the most, and not because he was a man. Well, sort of, but not in *that* way.

He was everything I wasn't: tall, masculine, built like an NFL linebacker, with a deep voice and skin as dark as espresso. For reference, I'm short, a pasty pink, and my masculinity is evaporating by the day. I look like Elton John, and sound like Nathan Lane.

None of that mattered.

We spent the 30-minute ride to the airport discussing life, my mom, and what unconditional love truly means.

When we got there, I unloaded his bags—and before I could step back, he pulled me into a giant bear hug—just pure gratitude and love.

I got back in the car, eyes wet, thinking, *I must be doing something right.*

I swear I heard Mom whisper, "That's my boy."

Since the 90s, I've had several experiences of oneness; this is now one of my most memorable.

Two strangers, zero differences—just unconditional love, right there at the terminal.

> *"The greatest joy in life is to love and be loved."*
> —Me, on the drive home that day

### Freer Than I've Ever Been

"How are you today?" one passenger asked. Without thinking, I responded,

"Freer than I've ever been!"

"Wow! That's huge." She said.

"I know, right?"

"How'd you get there?"

*How did I get here?*

In that moment, I realized something had shifted over the past few months.

"I'm realizing as I'm saying this that I've been living in a state of well-being I can only describe as this ongoing feeling of peace and joy happening simultaneously."

She smiled. "And what do you think brought this on?"

*Good question.* I wondered if she was a psychologist, with her rapid-fire, right-on-target questions. But I had an answer for her. I explained how I'd started putting Mom's lessons of unconditional love into practice, "...and this cocktail of peace and joy must be the result of doing so."

After I dropped her off, I turned off the ride-share app and sat there with a significant realization:

*Unconditional love—in action—is creating this feeling within me.*

### OMIGOSH! This is HUGE!

Throughout my adult life, I've been chasing *peace of mind* and *ongoing joy*. And now, I was finally experiencing both—for months, no less. It snuck up on me. And I wasn't even trying to achieve this!

*Could peace of mind and joy be the byproduct of living with unconditional love?*

I started to think it was.

# Love Has Side Effects?

Peace of mind. Lasting joy.

Those two things have evaded me most of my life. Yes, I have a long relationship with joy, but it seemed to come in spurts. Maybe I was confusing it with *happiness*, which tends to do just that. And peace of mind, on the other hand, I can assure you, left me after my carefree college days.

Even though I now realize that Mom had been living with peace and joy my entire life, I didn't know what they looked like. However, I was sure I'd recognize them when they arrived.

But, they never did. Trust me, I tried.

As I learned the hard way, peace and joy aren't something to be earned.

They're not goals I can work toward.

They're side effects.

How do I know?

I tried to achieve them for years—to no avail. They finally appeared when I lived with unconditional love as my intent and backed it with action.

After Mom died, when I started operating from a place of loving-kindness to *myself* and *others*, everything changed.

## Love First, Then Peace

Once I started practicing unconditional love—something shifted. My ride-share passengers noticed, even before I did.

I didn't get there by loving others instead of myself—that damn near killed me when I was caring for Mom. I got there by practicing patience and kindness with myself first.

It started by letting go of the stuff that robbed me of peace.

That's when the shift happened.

The magic didn't come from being "good."

It came from being gentle to myself.

I wasn't chasing peace.

I wasn't forcing joy.

I was just being patient and kind.

With myself.

Then it naturally extended to others.

And slowly—quietly—those two elusive visitors showed up.

Peace of mind settled in like a chair already molded to me.

Joy came, not as an ongoing high, but as a song in my heart and a whistle on my lips. That's when I know my heart is clear and my mind is free.

## What I Used to Think Joy Was

I used to think joy came with applause.

Success. Being wanted. Being seen.

I'd get flashes of it—moments of "I made it!"

But they vanished faster than the flames on your birthday candles and an overeager younger brother blowing them out first.

And I'd be back to chasing again.

Now, with several years of practicing unconditional loving-kindness?

The hurricane surrounds me, though I sit peacefully in its eye.

Love, peace, and joy quietly surround me in a hug.

My head is now filled mostly with what truly matters: something to do with what I love, and some silly song on repeat. I love that part.

## Happiness vs. Joy

I used to think being happy all the time was my only goal.

It hit me one day while watching *Willy Wonka and the Chocolate Factory*.

Happiness is fun, it's finding the Golden Ticket—a thrill! But short-lived.

Lasting joy is knowing you already have been given the keys to the Chocolate Factory—you belong there, forever. It's just there for you whenever you desire... or not. It's a constant.

And happiness? There's nothing wrong with happiness; it is a fun part of life. Even under the umbrella of lasing joy, it dances in and out on repeat.

When peace of mind and lasting joy show up together, it's like riding life's rollercoaster with an over-the-shoulder safety harness—fear, fun, twists, turns, and loop-de-loops—knowing I won't fly off the ride.

And for once, the statement,

"There's absolutely nothing going on between that boy's ears" feels like an accomplishment.

## The Byproduct is the Prize

If I had one banner to wave above everything I've learned so far, it would say this:

*Lasting peace and joy are the byproducts of unconditional love in motion.*

When I give it freely—when I live from within it—peace and joy are the prize in the Cracker Jack box.

Every time.

## What Money Can't Buy

Just like the Beatles song, "Money Can't Buy Me Love," it also can't buy peace of mind or lasting joy, either.

From what I can tell, most people today are either trying to regain their joy and peace, or they've never really experienced what either one feels like. And I'd bet that, right up there with the hunt for true love, peace of mind, and lasting joy are the most priceless things on the planet.

As I discovered, being surrounded by "things" won't bring peace and joy; they can't be bought—not with dollars, gold bars, or even crypto.

There may be other paths to peace, love, and joy, but the one I've found is paved with loving-kindness, and it costs nothing. That's priceless.

### The Polar Opposites of Peace of Mind and Lasting Joy

I've well established that I'm no scientist, but I've noticed through my bouts with anxiety and depression that they seem to be the polar opposites of peace of mind and lasting joy.

When I started following my joy—which, strangely enough, I found in country & western dancing—the depression began to lift. The more I nurtured that joy, the more I began to love myself, and the more it flowed outward towards others and back again.

By loving myself enough to curate what I let into my world, the anxieties quieted down—and peace of mind finally showed up to the party.

I haven't cracked the code, and I'm not sure that's the point, but I feel like what I'm doing is working for me, right now in this moment.

### I'm Not as Altruistic as I Might Sound

Now, while all this love, peace, and joy talk might feel noble and selfless, let's be clear:

I'm also really enjoying what I'm getting out of it.

Yes, I enjoy being kind, but I also appreciate the love I receive in return.

People are nicer. Life feels smoother.

Conversations are deeper. Laughter is louder.

And hugs? More frequent than ever—from perfect strangers.

It's like the universe has me on some loyalty rewards program:

"Thank you for loving generously. Please enjoy these side effects: inner peace, unexpected hugs, and free ongoing emotional upgrades."

So yes—I'm loving more. But I'm also getting more love in return, and I'm thrilled about it.

The more love I give, the more love I receive.

And if ongoing peace and joy are the byproduct of living with unconditional loving-kindness—count me in, make it a double.

## A Circle Back to Peaceful Delight

Earlier in the book, I used the term "Peaceful Delight" to describe my mom. It was also while writing this book, months later, that I realized this cocktail of peace of mind and lasting joy I'd been experiencing shared the same energy as Mom's.

That cocktail has a name: Peaceful Delight.

Yeah, I know you already put this together, but I hadn't.

I wanted to be more like Mom, and now I am.

# A Story Revealed in My Rearview

Why was I driving for a ride-share app?

Simply put: it felt good.

I enjoyed chatting with people, driving my car, getting paid for it, and paying my bills.

But between airport drop-offs and fifteen-minute therapy sessions, something happened.

People asked questions like those below, which naturally prompted responses about what was on my mind.

"What got you into driving?"

"What's the longest drive you've ever done?"

"What's a lesson you wish you'd learned earlier?"

"What's something that completely changed your perspective?"

"What's the nicest thing anyone's done for you on the road?"

Those all had *road trip* and *Mom's pearls* written all over them.

No matter how short the ride, I'd refer back to the same things:

What I'd learned. How I was finally living it. How it changed me.

And my story started showing up through the rearview mirror.

Before long, I'd shared my road trip story hundreds of times. Each time it struck a chord with these passengers. I could see it on their faces.

"Thank you—I needed that." "The world needs that reminder."

"Dude, you need to write a book!"

## Mom's Pearls Finally Landed

Mom's pearls landed, not just for me, but for every stranger sitting in my backseat who asked the right question and must've needed a reminder.

If I hadn't been driving, I wouldn't have put what I learned into words or seen the look in their eyes when something inside them clicked.

So I kept driving. Kept sharing. Kept writing.

Ride by ride, the story revealed itself.

Three years and over 5,500 rides later, I'm sitting here putting the final touches on my book.

I can see Mom's face with that glimmer in her eye, and hear her say, "That's my boy!"

# Mom Made It Last

## The Machine Worked—Until It Didn't

For years, I thought I had this whole "create your own life" thing nailed.
I'd read the books, built my Magical Manifesting Machine, and fueled it
with intention, grit, and confidence. It worked—I pulled off some wins
that even I couldn't believe.

But here's the thing: I could build success, but I couldn't make it last.

Somewhere along the line, something was missing.

## Tattoos Gone Wrong

Mabo, who is fluent in Japanese and Japanese kanji, feels bad for people
who get tattoos thinking they are one thing, when they are not. One poor
soul had a kanji tattoo, and Mabo asked what it meant, just to see what
they thought it was. "Oh, this means LOVE."

Mabo politely smiled, said "thank you," and walked away. He didn't have
the heart to tell them the truth: the symbol they had permanently
printed on them was *almost* correct. It was the basic outline for the word
LOVE, but the central part—the one that should represent the *heart*—was
missing. There was no space for it, and without it, their tattoo could
literally translate as "Heartless Love." That sounds like non-love.

It hit me. That was the same as me.

## The Missing Heart

As mentioned earlier in this book, my first self-affirming mantra was LASSO—calling forth Love, Abundance, Success, Serenity, and Opportunities. Love was right there in the front seat, driving the whole thing. Serenity was sitting in the passenger seat.

But as time went on, as my businesses and ambitions grew, love and serenity somehow fell by the wayside. Every "calling forth" during that era of my businesses was missing the one ingredient that mattered most, and its sidekick that made the ride better. Just like that person's tattoo, I was manifesting without heart—without love.

It wasn't until I started the "I love me" self-affirmations that love became central to my manifesting again.

Love wasn't just a missing piece—it was the proper fuel that turned my manifesting machine into something truly magical.

## Mom's the Glue

That's when Mom's pearls finally clicked into place—patience, kindness, compassion, and ultimately unconditional love.

Mom didn't teach me this in a lecture or a book—she showed me in a thousand little ways. By stretching powdered milk, five or more kids could have "real" cereal. By filling her meatloaf with a loaf of bread crumbs. By making government cheese casseroles that could feed an army of kids, whoever happened to be living with us that month. By always finding a way to make room for one more.

To her, love wasn't rationed; it was multiplied. She never said, "We don't have enough." Somehow, there was always enough.

And that became the glue.

I realized unconditional love isn't passive. It's not just a warm, fuzzy feeling floating out there. It's an action. It's fuel. It's the glue that holds everything in place.

## Love Lasts

I can see it clearly now:

What I built with fear? Failed.

What I built with ego? Evaporated.

What I built with love? Lasted.

When I manifest with love as my fuel—when I let patience and kindness steer me—the results don't just come, they last.

The love that Mom taught me made it last.

# A Oneness Massage

## Once Upon a Table

It wasn't until Mom's unconditional love started to sink in that I remembered something wild I'd experienced decades earlier. Back then, it felt important, but unexplainable. But now, the dots were starting to connect.

It all happened on a massage table.

And no, this is not the kind of story that starts with "happy" and ends with "ending." That story comes later. Yes, I'm afraid so.

In the mid-90s, I recall feeling somewhat envious of people who claimed to have experienced a sense of oneness. Growing up, I never felt anything like this in church, nor did I experience it while walking in nature. I wanted my moment too. So, I set an intention and, wouldn't you know it, I got exactly what I asked for.

About a month later, during a massage, I tried repeating "one" like a mantra, just to see what would happen. I'd never meditated in my life.

After a short while, I was in *it*. What "it" was, I couldn't explain—but I loved it. It felt as though the curtain had been pulled back on reality, everywhere and nowhere at once—all connected. I wasn't separate from anything. I was *love. It all was love*. Every person, every tree, every fleck of dust in the air—everything was me, connected. And it was all *love*.

The experience answered questions I didn't even know I had, and I knew it was essential. I understood some of it, but I knew there was so much more. For years, I filed it away under "weird mystical stuff I love, but can't explain."

## Until Mom's Pearls

Now, as I live more within unconditional love, I feel it flowing through everything, everywhere, all at once. And that's what oneness felt like that day on the massage table—a flow of love that was everything, everywhere, all at once.

Dink!

I'd carried that massage-table experience around for years without knowing what to do with it. Mom's pearls didn't erase it or replace it— they gave me the context. They made it click. What I'd felt back then as oneness, I was finally living now as unconditional love. And in that moment, I realized they weren't two separate things. They were the same.

Unconditional love = oneness.

Why does it matter? In this case, it matters because:

*What I do to you, I do to me. If I'm hating you, I'm hating me.*

*If I'm loving you, I'm loving me.*

Suddenly, it all made sense. The pieces of the puzzle fell into place. Mom helped me connect the dots between what I experienced on that table and what I was finally experiencing.

If the idea of *oneness* sounds *out there*, that's because *it is*. File your complaint with quantum physics. All I know is what I experienced.

---

*At reality's most fundamental level,*
*we're not separate—we're one.*
— paraphrasing physicist John Hagelin

---

I think we could use a bit of levity right about now. No, not levitating—a little chuckle to lighten the mood. Have I got a story for you!

## Speaking of Happy Endings… a true story

A friend of mine and her husband were in New York City and decided to get a massage. You know the type of place—off Times Square, 50 bucks each, plus "extras" if you're interested—this was 20 years ago. It turned out to be two tables shoved into a room, separated only by a sad shower curtain that looked like it had once lived in a Motel 1.0.

They're both lying there in silence with nothing but this curtain between them when, at the end of the session, she hears her husband's therapist lean in and whisper, "You want me to make banana cry? $20 extra."

Now—she's barely had time to process what that could possibly mean when her husband, without hesitation, breathes out, "Sur—"

As she tells it, he didn't even finish the word *sure* before she went airborne, while simultaneously ripping down the curtain and rod as she bellowed:

"There'll be *NO CRYING BANANAS TONIGHT!*"

Needless to say, there were no happy endings that night for either of them. She later found out he had a whole history of ongoing "happy endings." She ended the marriage, got free of the drama—and, in the ultimate twist, found her real happy ending—without him.

Wasn't that fun?

And yes, there's a moral to the story:

Never agree to a "happy ending" from your massage therapist with your spouse/significant other on the other side of a dirty shower curtain.

Now, wasn't that a fun, unexpected happy ending?

# Breaking "News"—I'm Breaking Up!

## The Noise

Breaking up is hard to do.

But boy, does it feel good.

Especially when it's with something that never loved me.

I'm not talking about a person.

I'm talking about the noise.

The 24/7 "news." The algorithms. The headlines.

The constant invitation to react, fear, divide, and defend.

I told myself I was "staying informed."

That it meant I cared.

That it made me responsible.

I allowed the noise to write my script.

And that script?

Made me angry. Anxious. Hopeless. Judgmental.

Pulled me away from people.

Convinced me I was "better than."

Robbed me of my peace.

That's not information.

That's poison.

Bye-Bye Bitches

So, I walked away.

From the noise. From the outrage. From the endless scroll.

Not for avoidance.

For my mental survival.

I gave myself permission to stop feeding the thoughts that harmed me.

I chose where I put my attention.

Patience.

Kindness.

Love.

It turns out the most radical kind of unconditional love...

is the kind I give to myself—it naturally extends to others.

## The Buttons Had to Go

I didn't grow up with buttons.

They came later—cable news and the internet's "greatest hits."

Before I knew it, I was full of buttons.

Judgment buttons.

Anger buttons.

Anxiety buttons.

Push any one of them—and BAM, there I went.

Now?

Those buttons are gone.

There's just space.

Curiosity. Compassion.

Sometimes just a chuckle.

I don't miss those buttons.

## Curating Peace

I started curating what I let in—media, conversations, self-talk, even people.

What life looks like now is simple:

Peaceful Delight.

No more negative charges firing off inside when I see or hear politics.

Just space where the buttons used to be.

A peaceful Jimmy changes more in this world than a fearful and judgmental Jimmy ever could.

So yes, I broke up with the noise.

We had a long run.

But in the end, it was simple.

"It's not you.

It's me.

I don't need you—

and that's best for me."

# Mom's Legacy

Mom didn't talk about unconditional love—she just lived it.

Because of that, she carried something rare: Peaceful Delight.

Well into my fifties, her life became a masterclass in love for me.

Better late than never.

My only regret is that I didn't fully enroll until after she passed away.

But once I listened to the pearls she'd hurled at my "pretty" little head, I finally understood.

She lived lovingly. No scorekeeping. No agenda.

Just love in motion.

And her love still teaches me.

It nudges me toward the same peace, joy, patience, and kindness she carried so effortlessly.

Her legacy lives in the patience I extend.

In the kindness I choose.

In the peace I curate.

She didn't leave me just memories—she left me a roadmap.

A legacy I get to live, share, and pass on.

# My Life Worth Loving

Mom didn't just love me. She taught me how to love myself—by living it.

It turns out I had no idea what unconditional love meant. Quite frankly, I never stopped long enough to give it much thought. The words were blended into the wallpaper of my youth—familiar, but meaningless. I never guessed that it started with me.

But it does.

The most essential piece—loving myself without conditions—was utterly lost on me.

I grew up thinking I had to earn love by becoming a better person.

Skinnier. Smarter. More successful. Attracted to women.

Less... me.

But I didn't have to become someone else to be loved.

I just had to stop running from the someone I already was.

And once I started practicing that—loving me, patiently and kindly—it all changed.

Turns out what I was chasing—peace of mind and joy—weren't lost treasures.

They were hanging out with love the whole time, rolling their eyes, waiting for me to show up.

They're not for sale.

They're the gift without purchase.

Mom's pearls weren't just about love—they were blueprints for building a life worth loving, and a world worth living in.

And yeah, it took me a while.

Here I am, finally getting what Mom tried to offer me all along:

Love isn't something you earn, hoard, or ration.

It's the current that connects us all.

It's why we're here.

That's my real-life fairy tale.

No knight.

No castle.

Just a boy who finally clicked his heels and realized...

*I'm home.*

And, according to my SASS Meter, I'm feeling like a Level 1.

So if you're out there trying to make your life worth living—I get it.

Here's what I found:

Make it a life worth loving first.

That's when peace and delight kick in.

Once I learned to love myself, I finally had both the ability—and the desire—to send love outward to others.

Not to change them. Not to fix them.

Just to love them.

The judgments quieted. The buttons disappeared.

Patience and kindness weren't just how I learned to treat myself—

They became how I now move through the world.

Build your yellow brick road as you wish.

Yours won't look like mine—it's not supposed to.

And those yellow bricks?

They're each stamped with the same Universal PSA—

**PLEASE BE PATIENT. PLEASE BE KIND**.

*"The greatest thing I've ever learned is to love—*

*and be loved in return."*

–Jimmy Belasco, paraphrasing *"Nature Boy"*

# A LITTLE CHALLENGE

"What could my life look like if I loved myself?"

You want something practical? Here it is.

Say "I love me" out loud.

Say it in your head.

Aim for a hundred times a day.

There's no magic number.

Do it for thirty days.

Sixty if you're an overachiever and really want to give it a go.

It's a Numbers Game

Say it... even if it feels empty.

...even if it feels stupid.

...even if it feels pointless.

This isn't magic.

It's just math.

And a little neuroscience—no big deal.

Repetition makes it work.

There's only an upside to this game.

Interested? Try it, see if it works for you.

Consider this a special gift with purchase.

Share your experiences:

Join our private fb page: theILOVEMEchallenge.com

# ACKNOWLEDGMENTS

To Mom, Dad, and my siblings—Geri Ann, John David, Susan, and Michael Todd—thank you for being my lifelong support system.

Mabo, you were the first person who made me truly want to put someone else before myself—and showed me how good that could feel. Thank you for quietly taking up the reins of unconditional love and stepping into Mom's shoes. Luckily, you wear the same size.

A deep, loving thank you to Mom #2 for sharing how Mom's love softened your heart and opened your mind. You started this entire process that helped me discover the power of unconditional love.

To my behind-the-scenes support team—Maggie, John, Mark-Brian, Joel, Gunner, Tami & Donald, Bill & Sandra, Hans, "Aunt" Nancy, Scott, Francesco, Kevin & Dwayne, and Jen—thank you for being there.

To those who read my rough drafts and had the nerve to tell me the truth—Jen, Holly, Anne, Debi, Gunner, and Scott—thank you!

To the group of teachers, staff, and administrators I worked alongside in the years after Mom's passing—thank you. You gave me more than a workplace; you gave me a place to heal—a three-year-long collective, unconditional love hug.

To my ride-share passengers—my captive audience—thank you. This story may never have made it onto paper if it hadn't first come to life through the countless times I shared it with you on those rides. Special thanks to those who asked for hugs—I felt loved. Especially to the man at the airport whose giant bear hug helped me realize *I must be doing something right*, and to the woman whose questions made me realize I was "freer than I've ever been" and how I got there.

And last, but surely not least, to all the rescue animals who opened my heart to selflessness and compassion—I send you my deepest love and gratitude. I look forward to seeing you again in Doggie & Kitty Heaven someday. I'll be the one who looks like a human, but loves like a dog.

# The Guy Behind the Tinted Lenses

Jimmy Belasco has been many things, among them: a soft-serve ice cream swirl specialist, a maker of pizzas and candles, and, more recently, a teacher's aide. He's also rescued more dogs than he can count, and one very cool cat named George.

These days, he's an over-enthusiastic storyteller, avid oversharer, and an occasional armchair philosopher who still believes in everyday magic.

He enjoys Pina Coladas, sunsets, and long walks on the beach with his husband, Mabo.

For more information or to contact Jimmy, visit: theJiMMYtalks.com

# Jimmy's SASS Meter (quick reference)

## LEVEL 1 – **Self-AWARENESS Surplus Stage** (SASS-1)

- Noticing other people exist and actually connecting with them
- Listening more, talking (slightly) less. It is possible.
- Your love, likability, and fabulousness factors are off the charts
- Showing patience & kindness to self and others—finally.
- Feels suspiciously like maturity, but let's not call it that.

## LEVEL 2 – **Self-ATTENTION Surplus Stage** (SASS-2)

- The spotlight is firmly on you—it's portable.
- Your self-controlled good lighting shows only your best angles.
- Hair, cars, clothes, social status: the fabulousness factor is high.
- Knowing others exist—mostly as your audience.
- "Delightfully tolerable"—somehow, people still like you.

## LEVEL 3 – **Self-ABSORPTION Surplus Stage** (SASS-3)

- Absorption Mode: image, success, and status are your oxygen.
- Your likability & fabulousness factors tank—you're barely tolerable.
- You're exhausting. To everyone—including yourself.
- You're too busy performing to notice any of this.
- Warning: Prolonged exposure may lead to Dark Periods and a diet of 99-cent double cheeseburgers and colas.

## LEVEL 4 – **Self-ABSORPTION "Syndrome" Stage** (SASS-4)

- You've crossed from "Surplus" into a self-imposed "Syndrome."
- You're just a jerk. Some might even call you an "Ass!"
- It's time for an intervention.
- Rescue a dog, or 13 dogs, and a cat named George. They'll place bets on who will outlive you. If you're lucky, you might learn to love like a dog before they win the bet.

## PHOTO CREDITS

www.ingramcontent.com/pod-product-compliance
Lightning Source LLC
Chambersburg PA
CBHW021029130626
46552CB00005B/1744